MW00783548

THE IRISH RITUAL OF CRAFT FREEMASONRY

as worked under Warrant of

THE GRAND LODGE OF IRELAND

Compiled for the use of the
Brethren as an Aide-Mémoire

By a Bro∴ Master Mason Belonging to the
IRISH CONSTITUTION

𝔓𝔬𝔢𝔪𝔞𝔫𝔡𝔯𝔢𝔰 𝔓𝔯𝔢𝔰𝔰
MASONIC PUBLISHERS
Boston & New York
1996

Kessinger Publishing's Rare Reprints
Thousands of Scarce and Hard-to-Find Books!

· · ·
· · ·
· · ·
· · ·
· · ·
· · ·
· · ·
· · ·
· · ·
· · ·
· · ·
· · ·
· · ·
· · ·
· · ·
· · ·
· · ·
· ·

We kindly invite you to view our extensive catalog list at:
http://www.kessinger.net

INTRODUCTION

In spite of the fact that daughter Lodges acting on Warrant under the Irish Constitution are required to practice the 'authorised working' of the Grand Lodge of Ireland, Grand Lodge has not seen fit to issue an authorised ritual text. Ritual uniformity is ostensibly maintained by a 'Grand Lodge of Instruction' which issues proclamations binding on its subordinate Lodges. As it stands, this system allows for variations in the ritual and one encounters, in difference locales, differences in the ceremonies.

An alleged ritual of the Irish workings was published some years ago in England,[1] but the text is verbally inaccurate, and it too much resembles the English 'Emulation-type' ceremonies. It does indeed include some features found in Ireland, but on the whole it is most untrustworthy and unreliable.

The present work, on the other hand, presents the ritual as it is conferred by the majority of Irish Lodges. One or two minor variations will be noted in the text, but the ceremonies are faithful to the actual workings of the average Irish Lodge. The author of this work is himself an active Irish Mason and has seen the ceremony performed countless times in numerous Lodges throughout the land. In addition to having been an active participant in the ceremonies of the three degrees, he has acquired the extensive notes of a deceased Past Master of his Lodge. These, coupled with his own experience and the review of four of his Brethren, insure that the text of the present work is an accurate copy of the ritual of the Irish Constitution.

---

[1] *The Irish Workings of Craft Masonry in the Three Symbolic Degrees* (London: A Lewis, 1957)

NOTES ON RITUAL PROCEDURE

Speak clearly and distinctly; do not give the impression that you are holding a confidential discussion with the Candidate. Remember that all the Brethren in the room desire to hear what you are saying.

Try to put the Candidate at ease. Ascertain that his Conductor directs him securely, but gently. Inasmuch as pain or injury can occur by allowing the Candidate to kneel on a small step, or a badly placed cushion, it is wise to test the kneeling stool yourself just prior to the meeting. It is not necessary that the Entered Apprentice step is actually the first of three. In this degree it is permissible for him to kneel on a kneeling stool or even on the floor. In the Fellowcraft and Master Mason degrees, however, the series of steps must be used.

Be considerate of the Candidate's physical posture. Do not keep him in any potentially unsettling or awkward position longer than absolutely necessary. For instance, after the Obligation is taken in the E.A. and F.C. degrees, the Candidate may kneel on both knees and in the F.C. degree his left arm may be dropped.

RULINGS OF THE GRAND LODGE OF IRELAND

The Master should always be addressed as 'Worshipful Master,' not as 'Worshipful Sir.' (Ref. 23)

The Conductor or Receiver of a Candidate is appointed by the Worshipful Master. (Ref. 34).

The Three Lesser Lights should be burning while conferring the three degrees. (Ref. 9).

After presenting Candidate to the Worshipful Master the Conductor does not ask the Worshipful Master his will and pleasure. (Ref. 9).

Brethren stand during the administration of all Obligations. (Ref. 53).

FIRST DEGREE
OPENING AN ENTERED APPRENTICES LODGE

The Director of Ceremonies will see that all the Officers of the Lodge are filled. If any of the Actual Officers are absent, then the vacant positions should be filled by some Past Masters for Wardens, and Master Masons for Lower Rank. The position of Worshipful Master can only be taken by the actual Worshipful Master or a Past Master. All Officers and Brethren stand until the Worshipful Master is seated.

WM—Let the Officers assume their places. Be seated, Brethren.

WM—Brother Inner Guard, close the door.

WM—⊢⊣ Rise, Brethren, and assist me to open the Lodge.

WM—⊢⊣ ⊢⊣ ⊢⊣

SW—⊢⊣ ⊢⊣ ⊢⊣

JW—⊢⊣ ⊢⊣ ⊢⊣

WM—Brother Junior Warden, what is the first care of a Mason in opening a Lodge?

JW—To see that the Lodge is tyled, Worshipful Master.

WM—See that duty performed.

JW—Brother Inner Guard, see that the Lodge is tyled.

IG—⊢⊣ ⊢⊣ ⊢⊣

TYLER—⊢⊣ ⊢⊣ ⊢⊣

IG—*Opens door.*

TYLER—Brother Inner Guard, the Lodge is tyled.

IG—(*shuts door*) Brother Junior Warden, the Lodge is tyled.

JW—Worshipful Master, the Lodge is tyled.

WM—Brother Senior Warden, what next demands our care?

SW—To see that each one present is in that Degree of Freemasonry on which the Lodge is about to be opened, Worshipful Master.

WM—How is that to be ascertained?

SW—By giving a word and exhibiting a Sign.

3

WM—Call the Deacons together, see that they are properly instructed, direct them to receive the word from each one present, and report the same to me.

SW—Let the Deacons approach.

Senior Deacon, carrying his wand in right hand, passes behind the chair of the Worshipful Master, proceeds along the South side of the Lodge to the Senior Warden, and halts at the right of the Senior Warden. The Junior Deacon, carrying his wand in right hand, passes behind the Chair of the Senior Warden and halts in front of and at the left of the Senior Warden. The Senior Deacon whispers the word to the Senior Warden, who instructs him to take the word from the Brethren in the South and Brethren on the Dais to the left of the Worshipful Master. The Junior Deacon, in like manner, gives the word to the Senior Warden, and is instructed to take the word from the Brethren in the North, and Brethren on the Dais to the right of the Worshipful Master. When the word is taken from all present, the Senior Warden gives the word to the Worshipful Master, and then waits at the foot of the Dais, until the Junior Deacon gives the word to the Worshipful Master. When this is done the Deacons return at once to their respective positions. If the chairs of the Worshipful Master and Senior Warden are fixed against the walls of the room, the Deacons will pass in front of the Worshipful Master and Senior Warden respectively.

WM—Brethren, I have received the word.

WM—Brother Junior Warden, direct the Brethren to stand to order in that Degree of Freemasonry on which the Lodge is about to be opened.

JW—Brethren, it is the will and pleasure of the Worshipful Master that you do stand to order in that Degree of Freemasonry on which the Lodge is about to be opened.

The Brethren give the Sign, Junior Warden satisfies himself that each Brother is standing to Order correctly.

4

JW—Worshipful Master, the Brethren have given me the Sign.

WM—Which I acknowledge to be correct, and thus ratify it.

The Junior Warden gives the 'standing to order' Sign, the Worshipful Master gives it also, and finishes with the full Salute which is likewise given by all the Brethren.

WM—Brother Inner Guard, where is your place in the Lodge?

IG—Inside the Door of the Porch.

WM—What is your duty there?

IG—To answer all regular knocks, to admit none but Brethren properly clothed and Candidates duly prepared, to announce the name and rank of each Visiting Brother, and to suffer none to enter or depart, save at the will and pleasure of the Worshipful Master.

When the Inner Guard is giving his answer he will stand to order, the same applies to every other Officer following. When finished stating the duty, the Officer salutes the Worshipful Master.

WM—Brother Junior Deacon, where is your place in the Lodge?

JD—At the back of the chair of the Senior Warden, or at his right hand, if so permitted.

WM—What is your duty there?

JD—To carry all messages from the Senior Warden to the Junior Warden, and to distribute the same throughout the Lodge if so directed.

WM—Brother Senior Deacon, where is your place in the Lodge?

SD—At the back of the chair of the Worshipful Master, or at his right hand, if so permitted.

WM—What is your duty there?

SD—To carry all messages from the Worshipful Master to the Senior Warden, and to distribute the same throughout the Lodge if so directed.

The Deacons, when answering, will transfer their wands to their Left hand so as to stand to order and salute.

WM—Brother Junior Warden, where is your place in the Lodge?

JW—In the South.

WM—What is your duty there?

JW—The better to observe the Sun on the Meridian. To call the Brethren from Labour to refreshment and on again to Labour, so that pleasure and profit may result therefrom.

WM—Brother Senior Warden, where is your place in the Lodge?

SW—In the West.

WM—What is your duty there?

SW—As the Sun sets in the West to close the glorious day, so the Senior Warden stands in the West, to close the Lodge, at the will and pleasure of the Worshipful Master.

WM—Brother Immediate Past Master (*or any Past Master*), where is the Master's place in the Lodge?

IPM—In the East.

WM—What is his duty there?

IPM—As the Sun rises in the East to open and illumine the glorious day, so the Worshipful Master presides in the East to open the Lodge, to rule and govern it with good and wholesome instruction, or in his unavoidable absence to appoint a fit and proper Brother so to do.

WM—It is so. I acknowledge my place and duty.

WM—Let the Wardens declare to the Brethren, that it is my will and pleasure that the Lodge do now open.

SW—Brethren, it is the will and pleasure of the Worshipful Master that the Lodge do now open.

Whilst the Wardens are making this declaration the Deacons, Director of Ceremonies, and Chaplain will assemble at the Altar. The Senior Deacon standing at the South side, the Junior Deacon at the North side, the Director of Ceremonies and Chaplain at the West of the

6

Altar facing the Worshipful Master must wait until these positions are taken up.

WM—Accordingly, Brethren, in the name of the Most High God, the Great Architect of the Universe, I declare the Lodge to be now open, and at Labour on this the First or Entered Apprentice Degree of Freemasonry, for the transaction of all such business as may be regularly brought before it. Your Entrance Phrase being: 'By the help of God, and the tongue of good report' and this — (*making the sign*) your True Guard and Sign.

At the words, 'I declare the Lodge to be now open,' the Deacons will raise their wands, and bring same to the coping position over the Three Great Lights. The Director of Ceremonies will arrange the Three Great Lights in proper position. The Wardens will reverse the Pillars on the tables or pedestals, that of the Junior Warden being put down, and that of the Senior Warden put up.
The Prayer is read, or recited by the Chaplain.

WM—❙ —❙ —❙
SW—❙ —❙ —❙
JW—❙ —❙ —❙
IG—❙ —❙ —❙
TYLER—❙ —❙ —❙

All the Brethren (except the Deacons) salute the Worshipful Master.
If an Hymn or Ode is sung, it is sung at this point. The Deacons, Director of Ceremonies, and Chaplain remain at the Altar until it is finished.

WM—Be seated, Brethren.

Business of the Lodge meeting then proceeds.

7

FIRST DEGREE
OR
CEREMONY OF INITIATION

It is recommended that the Director of Ceremonies should retire from the Lodge room, and assist in the Preparation of the Candidate. When the Candidate is ready the usual Knocks are given by the Tyler.

N.B.—In preparing the Candidate the Cable Tow is placed THREE times around the neck.

IG—Worshipful Master, there is an alarm at the Candidate's Porch.

If there is not a special door for Candidates, the Inner Guard will use the following:—

IG—Worshipful Master, there is an alarm at the door of the Porch.
WM—Ascertain the cause thereof.

Inner Guard knocks on door, waits until answered by the Knocks from without. Inner Guard opens door, receives the information from the Tyler, and closes the door.

IG—One in darkness who wishes to approach the Light, and to receive some of the Rights and Privileges of Freemasonry, as many good and true men have done before.
WM—How does he hope to obtain so great an honour?

Inner Guard Knocks on the door, waits until answered by the knocks from without. Inner Guard opens the door, receives the information from the Tyler and closes the door.

IG—By the help of God, and the Tongue of Good Report.
WM—What good can be reported of him?

8

Inner Guard Knocks on the door, waits until answered by the knocks from without. Inner Guard opens the door, receives the information from the Tyler and closes the door.

IG—That he is a man, free-born, without maim or defect, living in good repute amongst his friends and neighbours.

WM—His name, age, and occupation?

Inner Guard Knocks on the door, waits until answered by the knocks from without. Inner Guard opens the door, receives the information from the Tyler and closes the door.

IG—Mr. — — full Masonic age, Printer (*or whatever the correct name and occupation may be*).

WM—Admit him.

Inner Guard Knocks on the door, waits until answered by the knocks from without. Inner Guard opens the door, and admits the Candidate who is now taken in charge by the Conductor. Inner Guard closes the door. The Conductor leads the Candidate to the North West Corner, that is, to the left of the Senior Warden, and halts the Candidate in front of a kneeling cushion. By this time the Deacons will be in position, the Senior Deacon to the left of the Candidate, and the Junior Deacon to the right. The Chaplain will have the appropriate Prayer ready and may stand at the Altar or near the Candidate if more convenient.

COND.—Mr. — —, we believe that for the first time in your life you now stand within a Lodge of Freemasons in which the Brethren are engaged in their peculiar labour. By the direction of the Worshipful Master, I have to put to you certain questions to which we expect straightforward and truthful answers: —

1. Do you come here of your own free-will and accord, unbiased by improper solicitation of friends, and uninfluenced by any mercenary or other unworthy motive?

2. Do you come with a preconceived notion of the excellence of our Order, a desire for knowledge, and to make yourself more extensively useful amongst your fellow-men?

3. Will you cheerfully conform to the established customs and usages of the Fraternity?

Can.—*Replies.*

Conductor then places the point of the Hostile Weapon at the Candidate's breast.

COND.—Do you feel anything?

Can.—I do.

COND.—It is the point of a Dagger. As this pricks your flesh, so may the remembrance prick your conscience should you at any time be tempted to betray the trust we are now about to place in you.

COND.—(*turning toward Worshipful Master*) Worshipful Master, the Candidate has been received according to Ancient Custom.

WM—Let him kneel, and receive the benefit of prayer.

Excepting the Candidate, all the Brethren rise. Chaplain reads the prayer.

WM—Mr. —, in the hour of difficulty and danger, in whom do you put your trust?

Can.—In God.

WM—Let him who puts his trust in God arise, follow his Conductor, fearing no evil.

Candidate now rises, and is led by the Conductor three times round the Lodge Room, the Deacons walking in front. First time around, going behind the chairs of the Junior and Senior Warden; second time round, stop at the chair of the Junior Warden. Conductor takes the Candidate's Right Hand, and with it gives the knocks of the Degree on the Right Shoulder of the Junior Warden, who says:—

JW—Who comes here?

COND.—One in darkness who wishes to approach the Light, and to receive some of the Rights and Privileges of Freemasonry, as many good and true men have done before.

JW—How does he hope to obtain so great an honour?

COND.—By the help of God, and the Tongue of Good Report.

JW—What good can be reported of him?

COND.—That he is a man, free-born, without maim or defect, living in good repute amongst his friends and neighbours.

JW—Let him enter.

The Junior Warden does NOT ask for his name, age, and occupation. The Junior Warden now pushes forward his table (or pedestal), and when possible the Conductor leads the Candidate forward between the Junior Warden and the table (or pedestal). Meanwhile, the Deacons have proceeded to the far side of the Junior Warden and are ready to go in front of the Conductor and Candidate. The procession passes behind the Chair of the Senior Warden and on arriving before the Worshipful Master, the Conductor halts the Candidate facing him towards him. The Deacons stand at both sides of the Conductor and Candidate; the Senior Deacon to the left, the Junior Deacon to the right.

COND.—Worshipful Master, I present to you this Candidate for Freemasonry; he has duly entered the Southern Gate.

WM—Take him to the Senior Warden, and crave his fraternal assistance in having the Candidate placed in the proper position in order to take an Obligation.

The Senior Deacon goes forward and joins the Junior Deacon, all proceed to the front of the Senior Warden, about one pace from the Altar and face the Senior Warden. The Deacons stand a little to the side; the Senior Deacon to the South side, the Junior Deacon to the North side.

COND.—Brother Senior Warden, by direction of the Worshipful Master, I present to you this Candidate for Freemasonry, and crave your fraternal assistance in having him placed in the proper position to take an Obligation.

SW—Let the Candidate stand erect, and face the East.

The Conductor turns the Candidate right, so that he faces the Altar. Deacons also turn and face the East.

SW—Let him take one step forward with the Left Foot, placing the heel of the Right Foot in the Hollow of the Left Foot, forming a Square.

Let him kneel on the Left Knee on the first of a series of steps, squaring the Right Leg.

Let him place his Left hand under the Volume of the Sacred Law[2] and his right over the same and certain emblems thereon.

The Conductor assists the Candidate in these movements.

COND.—Worshipful Master, the Candidate is now in the proper position to take the Obligation.

---

[2] The Volume of the Sacred Law must be a religious work of the Candidate's faith; e.g., the Bible, Quran, Vedas, etc.

WM—Mr. —, as we are now about to communicate to you the secrets peculiar to this degree, we require you to take an Obligation of secrecy.

With regard to this Obligation, I give you my assurance that there is nothing in it at variance with your religious belief, political opinion, the allegiance you owe to your Sovereign or the Rulers of the State to which you belong. Nor is there anything in it hurtful to your feelings as a man of honour.

I further assure you that, with the exception of yourself, everyone here present has already taken this Obligation.

Having this assurance from me, are you now willing to take this Obligation, and by it become bound to us, as we are to one another?

Can.—I am.

WM—Since none by the free can take a voluntary Obligation, I now symbolically release you.

Here the Halter[3] is taken off the Candidate.

OBLIGATION

I, ——, of my own free-will and accord, in the presence of the Most High God, the Great Architect of the Universe, and of this worthy, worshipful and warranted Lodge of Ancient, Free and Accepted Masons, regularly constituted, properly assembled and duly dedicated in His Most Holy Name, do hereby—*Conductor lightly raises the Candidate's right hand*—and hereon—*Conductor replaces the Candidate's right hand*—solemnly and sincerely promise, vow and declare that I will ever hele, conceal, and never will reveal unlawfully, aught of the hidden points, secrets, or mysteries of, or belonging to, Ancient Craft Masonry, which have been heretofore, shall now, or may hereafter become known to me in any way whatsoever.

---

[3] According to the Irish Constitution, the Candidate wears a Halter, NOT a 'Cable Tow.' The Cable Tow is a symbol of the 'traveling distance' a Brother is bound by to fulfill his Obligations.

I will not communicate, divulge or discover these secrets to anyone in the whole world except to him or to them to whom the same do surely, justly and of right belong, that is to say, in the body of a Lodge of Freemasons just, perfect and regular, or to a well-known Brother Freemason, or to one who is duly vouched to me at the mouth of a well-known brother, or to one whom after due trial and strict examination I shall find to be lawfully entitled to the same.

I will not write or print, or in any way delineate those secrets on anything moveable or immovable beneath the canopy of heaven whereby or whereon any letter, character or symbol, or even the least trace thereof may become unlawfully known legible or intelligible to myself or anyone else in the whole world through my inadvertence, negligence or misconduct.

All these points I solemnly promise, vow and declare that I will observe without any evasion, equivocation or mental reservation whatsoever, bearing in mind the ancient penalty of having the t.c.a., the t.t.o. at the rs. and b. in the r.ss. of the s., a cable's length from the s., where the t.es. and fs. twice daily, and binding myself under the real penalty of being deservedly branded as a wretch, base, faithless and unworthy to be received among men of honour, should I knowingly or willfully violate in letter or spirit this my most solemn, sincere and voluntary Obligation as an Entered Apprentice Freemason.

WM—You will now ratify the Obligation you have just taken by kissing the Volume of the Sacred Law, which lies between your hands or in any other manner equally binding on your conscience.

Candidate ratifies, and Worshipful Master continues:—

WM—Having been for sometime in a state of darkness, of what do you most stand in need of?
Can.—Light.
WM—And God said, 'Let there be Light, and there was Light.'

The Conductor will slowly remove the Hoodwink, placing his right hand over the brow of the Candidate, so that the Candidate will look upon the Volume of the Sacred Law.

WM—The first object that meets your eyes in a Masonic Lodge is the Volume of the Sacred Law on which you took your solemn Obligation in darkness. That Volume of the Sacred Law is the book known to us as the [Holy Bible].[4] We ask you to assure yourself that it is the [Holy Bible], and if you are satisfied, will you once again ratify the Obligation, this time in the Light, in a like manner as you did in the darkness.

Candidate does so.

By this time some of the Brethren have gathered round the Altar, facing the Candidate. Some hold their swords or daggers pointed towards the Candidate, while other Brethren extend their right hands. The Worshipful Master does NOT leave his seat.

COND.—Brother — (for as such am I now permitted to address you) Freemasonry may be described as a peculiar system of morality, veiled in allegory and illustrated by symbols, so that everything done in this, the ceremony of your Initiation, has its symbolic significance and Masonic meaning.

I would first ask you to observe the attitude of the Brethren assembled round this Altar. Some have hostile weapons pointed towards your naked and defenseless breast, indicative of the undying hostility which would pursue you, should you ever prove false to your Obligation. Others have the right hand extended to you, signifying that as long as you prove true to your Obligation the 'Right Hand of Masonic Fellowship' will ever be held out to greet you. But, believing that you will prove a true and trusty Brother amongst us, I ask the Brethren, who are holding the hostile weapons, to lay them aside and, with the other Brethren, extend to you the

---

[4]'Holy Bible' may be replaced by 'Quran,' suiting the needs of the Candidate.

right hand, thus assuring you of a welcome into our Order as a Brother Freemason.

The Brethren now resume their seats. The Conductor waits until all is quiet and then continues:—

COND.—On this Altar before you are the 'Lights of Freemasonry,' known to us as the 'Three Great Lights,' and the 'Three Lesser Lights.'

The Three Great Lights lie between your hands. They are, the Volume of the Sacred Law, the Square, and the Compasses.

The Volume of the Sacred Law is recommended to your consideration and study without comment, believing that if you will follow its teaching and precepts, you will find them a 'Light to your feet, and a Lamp to your Path.'

The Square is an emblem of Morality, and teaches us that all our actions towards our fellow men should stand the test of the Moral Square.

The Compasses, which form that perfect figure the Circle, remind us that we should endeavour to surround our conduct by a line to keep in check unruly passions and unlawful desires.

This, the Three Great Lights teach the Freemason his duty to God, to his neighbour and to himself.

The Three Lesser Lights are represented by the three tapers burning before you. That on the left represents the Sun, which rules the day; that on the right, the Moon which governs the night; and that in the East, the presiding officer of the Lodge, who is called the Worshipful Master. As the Sun and Moon perform their duty regularly and harmoniously according to the unaltering laws of Nature, so they remind the Worshipful Master that his work in the Lodge should be done in a like manner. When we assemble together to take part in our meetings or, as we call it, 'Labour,' we all meet, for the time being, strictly on a Fraternal Level, without distinction or outside Rank. We meet as Brethren, but we are permitted to elect from our company one who shall preside over our assemblies for a period of twelve months, and that Brother is given the title

Worshipful Master. During his term of Office his rulings must be implicitly employed, his decisions cannot be questioned in open Lodge, but if at any time you consider that an unfair decisions has been given, or that you have not had just treatment, there is a higher authority in our Order to which you may bring your complaint; that authority is known as the Grand Lodge of Ireland, the governing body over all the Lodges under the jurisdiction of the Irish Constitution of Freemasonry.

It is possible that you may have heard Freemasonry described as a Secret Society by people who know nothing of our teaching and principles, or who are not in sympathy with us. But I can assure you that Freemasonry is NOT a secret society, as our meeting places are well known to the Rulers of the State in which we reside. Our laws and Constitution are published and may be obtained and read by any person who so desires, and further there is nothing in our teaching in any way contrary to the religious or political opinion of any man, nor is there anything contrary to the law of the land in which we reside. In fact, so careful are we that nothing of this nature shall arise, it is a fundamental rule in our Order that no discussion upon Religion or upon Politics is permitted either at Labour in the Lodge meeting, or at the refreshment board. But, Freemasonry is a society possessing secrets which are used as a means of recognition amongst its members. It is my privilege, as well as duty, now to communicate some of those secrets to you.

We are known to one another by Sound, by Touch and by Sight. In Sound, by Knocks and Words; in Touch, by grips; and by Sight, by certain regular Signs.

The Knocks of the Degree are given thus: —▮ —▮ —▮. Should you, at any time, find yourself outside the closed door of a Masonic Lodge, and hear these Knocks given on the door, you will understand that within there is a Lodge at Labour on this, the Entered Apprentice Degree.

To gain admission to a Lodge meeting, it is necessary to be in possession of what is known to us as 'The Word.' Strictly speaking, it is a Phrase. You have heard this given on your behalf twice during the earlier part of the Ceremony. It is, 'By the help of God, and the tongue of good report.'

It is important to remember this Phrase, because without it you would not be permitted to remain in the Lodge Room for the Opening Ceremony. At a certain time in this Opening two of the Officers, called Deacons, will be instructed to that 'The Word' or Entrance Phrase from each one present, and when one of the Deacons comes to you, you will quietly whisper this Entrance Phrase, when he will be satisfied that you are qualified to remain in the room. To impress this important Phrase on your memory I shall give you a brief account of the manner of your election into Freemasonry.

Your name was proposed and seconded in what we call Open Lodge similar to our present assembly. Certain Brethren were appointed to make inquiries as to your suitability and fitness for Membership.

At the next meeting these Brethren reported favourably on your behalf, a ballot was taken, which proved unanimous. So strict is our method of election that one Black Bean or adverse vote would have disqualified you for immediate admission. You will thus understand that we are all here 'By the help of God, and the tongue of good report.'

The Secret Word of this degree is accompanied by a certain handshake or 'Grip.' If you are under examination proving yourself to be an Entered Apprentice Freemason there is a certain method by which that Word and Grip may be given, which I will now illustrate with the assistance of a well-instructed Brother.

Conductor now asks one of the Brethren of the Lodge to come forward. The Conductor gives the Covered Grip of an Entered Apprentice, and says to the Brother:—

COND.—What is this?
BRO.—A Grip in Freemasonry.
COND.—(*to Candidate*) Brother — —, can you see the Grip?
Can.—No.

18

COND.—(*to well-instructed Brother*) What is the use of a Mason's left hand?

BRO.—To cover his work.

COND.—(*to Candidate*) Brother ——, under the Irish Constitution, it is our practice to impart Grips with the right hand while covering them with the left; but, for the purpose of your instruction, and as a demonstration for your benefit on the occasion of your Initiation, this Grip is now given uncovered that you may see the proper manner in which it is to be given.

The Conductor then teaches the Candidate the Grip and Word, explaining the same, and reminding him that it must always be given 'covered.'

COND.—(*to Candidate*) Brother ——, you heard the question, 'What is the use of a Mason's left hand?' To this our Brother responded, 'To cover his work.' In some Lodges you will find Brethren who respond 'To hele the Grip,' or 'To cover the work.' Any of these responses will do.

COND.—(*to well-instructed Brother*) Wherein did you receive this Grip?

BRO.—In the Body of a Lodge, Just, Perfect, and Regular.

COND.—Why Just?

BRO.—Because the Volume of the Sacred Law is exposed on the Altar.

COND.—Why Perfect?

BRO.—Because seven Brethren are present.

COND.—Why Regular?

BRO.—Because the Warrant of the Lodge is here with us.

COND.—Whereon did you receive this Grip?

BRO.—Kneeling on the first of a series of Steps.

COND.—Whereby did you receive it?

BRO.—By virtue of a Obligation.

COND.—Did you receive anything with this Grip?

BRO.—Yes, I received a Word.

COND.—Will you give me that Word?

BRO.—No, at my Initiation I was taught caution, but I will letter it or halve it with you.

COND.—Begin.

BRO.—No, you being the challenger, must begin.

The Word is then spelt alternately letter by letter by the Conductor and the well-instructed Brother, and then pronounced by its two syllables.

The Conductor then repeats the foregoing dialogue with the Candidate, and impresses upon him the necessity for caution when asked for the Word.

The Conductor also explains that the Word and Grip are not ordinarily used in the Ceremonies of the Lodge.

COND.—With this Word (*giving it*) and this Grip, I assist you to arise from the kneeling position, as a duly obligated Brother Entered Apprentice Freemason.

The Signs of the Degree are the Due Guard, and the True Guard, or Salute. A few moments ago you were instructed how to advance to the Altar in order to take an Obligation. Place your feet as so directed, and your hands as if in the position of taking the Obligation. (*Conductor goes through the movement, at the same time directing the Candidate to repeat same.*) You are now standing with the Sign of the Due Guard, meaning that the secrets communicated to you will be well and truly guarded by you. The Sign of the Due Guard is not used in our ceremonies under the Constitution of Ireland. It is, however, used elsewhere and might be asked for if you were undergoing examination. You may now drop both hands to your sides.

Again, paying attention to the position of the Feet (*Conductor places his own feet in position and directs Candidate to do likewise.*) and calling to mind the ancient penalty referred to in the Obligation, you give the Salute or True Guard as follows: (*Conductor explains and directs the Candidate to follow the movements*). Should you at any time address the Worshipful Master, you would give him this Salute when you rise to speak or, when crossing the floor of the Lodge room, you would halt when passing the Worshipful Master, face him and salute as instructed, and then proceed across the room.

At a certain part of the Opening Ceremony of the Lodge meeting, the Brethren will be instructed to stand to Order in that Degree on which the Lodge is about to be opened. You would stand with your feet thus, as already explained, and with your right hand give the first part of the Salute, and wait until it is ratified by the Worshipful Master. Then you complete the Sign, thus: (*Demonstrating.*)

Now, referring to the Obligation: this may be summed in one word, and that is SECRECY. You will note that you took this Obligation in the presence of the Most High God, 'The Great Architect of the Universe,' for as such is the Deity referred to in this Degree.

Secrecy is impressed upon you. Therefore, you will be specially careful not to discuss or communicate the information you have received with anyone, except those lawfully entitled thereto.

There are four exceptions. Firstly, to one whom you meet in the body of a Lodge of Freemasons, Just, Perfect, and regular, as we are meeting here now, so that you recognise each person present as a Brother Entered Apprentice Freemason.

Secondly, to a well-known brother Entered Apprentice Freemason, and that means a Brother whom you have met in a Lodge at labour.

Thirdly, to one vouched to you at the mouth of a well-known Brother Freemason. Masonic voucher can be done only, as we say, 'by word of mouth.' That is to say, it must be done in the presence of all concerned. You cannot vouch one Brother to another by writing a letter to that effect, nor can you point to a certain person and say, 'that man (Buck Mulligan) is a Brother Freemason.' Let me illustrate this: I meet you in town, say, I know you are a Brother Freemason as I have met you in a Lodge at labour. Whilst we are talking, another man joins us whom I also know to be a

Brother Freemason, because I have met him in a Lodge at labour. Therefore I am perfectly in order and can vouch you to this man as a Brother Entered Apprentice Freemason. Thus only can you vouch by word of mouth in the presence of all concerned.

Fourthly, by examination, proving to your satisfaction that the stranger is a Freemason. As you have yet a considerable amount to learn in Masonic matters, we ask you NOT to be tempted to test strangers upon Masonic matters, but rather to wait until you are better instructed as to the correct method of an examination.

You have promised that you will not write any of the secrets which have been communicated to you. By the secrets we mean the Words, Signs and Grips. Nor may you give a description of the same by intelligible means, such as depicting or drawing. For by doing so, you are liable to the punishment of suspension from your Lodge, and, although it is not exactly expressed in your Obligation, yet we ask you to do all in your power to prevent anyone else unlawfully communicating our secrets.

The Obligation closes by calling to mind the Ancient Penalty meted out to the traitor, and the more real Penalty of being deservedly branded as a wretch and unfit for the society of men of honour, should you ever knowingly or willfully violate aught of this, your solemn, sincere, and voluntary Obligation, being that of an Entered Apprentice Freemason.

When you entered into the Tyler's Room to be prepared for Initiation, almost every action in that preparation was symbolic in its meaning.

Firstly, you were divested of your money, jewelry and all articles of metal to impress upon you that all Candidates enter the Order strictly on a Level, and for their moral worth as men.

Secondly, you were divested of most of your clothing, your left breast was bared in token of sincerity of your intention. Your right arm was bared, meaning that you are willing to work for Freemasonry. Your left knee was bared in token of humility. You were slipshod, representing an ancient custom of ratifying a contract or bargain as the practice of the Hebrews. A Halter was placed around your neck in token of submission to the ordeal of Initiation, and you were blindfolded representing one in darkness, wishing to approach the Light; that is, the Light of Masonry, which explains the first announcement by the Tyler on announcing your admission into the Lodge Room.

The second announcement by the Tyler, stating that you were a 'man, free-born' may seem strange to you. But it will remind you that in years gone by there were slaves in our land, and men who were under the power of an Overlord (Slaves and Bondsmen who had no free will of their own), thus impressing on you the antiquity of the Order of Freemasonry. No Slave or Bondsman could be admitted, nor can any man be coerced into joining our Order. The Candidate must enter of his own free will and accord.

WORKING TOOLS

Now, from what you have heard of Freemasonry in general, you will realise that although we call ourselves Masons, yet we do not take part in any manual labour as performed by the Operative Mason. But, we do use certain implements of the Operative Mason to impress upon us moral lessons, and these implements are called the Working Tools of the Degree. The Working Tools of the Entered Apprentice Degree are the Twenty-four inch Gauge and the Common Gavel.

The Twenty-four inch Gauge is an implement twenty-four inches long, divided by marks into twenty-four equal parts. The Operative Mason uses it to bring the work he is engaged upon to the required dimensions. It has been adopted in Speculative Masonry to represent the twenty-four hours of the day by its main divisions; hence, its symbolic use is to teach us so to dispose of our daily life, that we may spend a part in our usual vocations, part in rest and recreation, not forgetting a part in the service of our Creator. In the symbolic language of Freemasonry, the Twenty-four inch Gauge becomes the symbol of Time, well-spent.

The Common Gavel is made use of by the Operative Mason to knock off the corners and excrescences of the Rough Stone, and thus fit it better for the builder's use. It has been adopted in Speculative Masonry as a symbol to admonish us of the duty of divesting our minds and consciences of all the vices and impurities of life, thereby fitting ourselves as living stones for that spiritual building, not made with hands, eternal in the Heavens.

The Candidate is now brought before the Worshipful Master and invested with the Apron. He is then placed in the Northeast corner of the Lodge Room while the Charge is read to him.

CHARGE TO A NEWLY-MADE BROTHER

Brother, as you have now gone through the Ceremony of Initiation, allow me to congratulate you on being admitted, by the unanimous consent of the Lodge, a member of our ancient and honourable society; ancient, as embodying principles that have existed from time immemorial; and honourable, as tending to make all those honourable who are strictly obedient to its precepts. No institution can boast a more solid foundation than that on which Freemasonry rests—'the practice of social and moral virtue.' And to so high an eminence has its credit been advanced, that even monarchs have become promoters of the Craft, have not thought it beneath them to exchange the Sceptre for the Trowel, have become members of our society, and have taken part in our assemblies.

As a Freemason, I would first recommend to your most serious contemplation the Volume of the Sacred Law, charging you to consider it as the unerring standard of truth and morals, and to regulate your actions by the Divine precepts it contains. Thereby you will learn how to discharge your duty to God, by never mentioning His Name save with the awe and reverence that are due from a creature to the Creator: by imploring His aid on all your undertakings, and by looking up to Him on every emergency for comfort and support; to your neighbor, by acting towards him uprightly, by rendering him every kind office that justice or mercy may require, by sympathising in his distress, by soothing his afflictions, and by always doing to him as you would he should do unto you; to yourself, by such a prudent and well-regulated course of discipline as may tend to preserve your faculties in their fullest energy, and may enable you to exert most usefully the talents with which God has blessed you, as well to His glory as to the welfare of your fellow-creatures.

As a Citizen, I enjoin you to be exemplary in the discharge of your civil duties, by never proposing or countenancing anything which may disturb the peace and good order of society; by paying obedience to the laws of the State in which you reside, and by which you are protected, and by never losing sight of the allegiance you owe to the sovereign of your native land.

As an individual, I would enjoin upon you the practice of every domestic as well as public virtue. Let Prudence direct you, temperance chasten you, Fortitude support you, and Justice be the guide of all your actions. Bear constantly in mind the indispensable duties of Candour, Discretion, and Fidelity; and be especially careful to maintain in their fullest vigour those truly Masonic characteristics: benevolence and Brotherly-love.

The Candidate is now seated in the Northeast corner and saluted.

CLOSING AN
ENTERED APPRENTICES LODGE

WM—Brother Secretary, have you any further business to submit?

SECY—Worshipful Master, there is no further business for consideration.

WM—Brethren, as I am about to close the Lodge, has any Brother, a member of the Lodge, anything to say for the good of Freemasonry in general or this Lodge in particular?

At this point Candidates may be proposed; notices of motion handed in, etc.

WM—Brethren, as I am about to close this Lodge, has any visiting Brother anything to say for the good of Freemasonry in general, or this Lodge in particular?

Visiting Brethren may now extend fraternal greetings from their respective Lodges, and make other appropriate remarks.

WM—Brethren of the Lodge, rise and assist me to salute our visiting Brethren.

The Salute is given according to the highest rank of the visiting Brethren. Visiting Brethren should stand and salute the Worshipful Master, and then all Brethren resume their seats.

WM—Brethren, as I am about to close the Lodge, has any Brother anything to say for the good of Freemasonry in general, or this Lodge in particular?

At this point any Brother may speak regarding any Lodge matters which may have been overlooked. If a light refreshment is to follow the meeting, the Junior Warden announces the same.

At this point any Brother may speak regarding any Lodge matters which may have been overlooked. If a light refreshment is to follow the meeting, the Junior Warden announces the same.

WM——✸ Rise, Brethren, and assist me to close the Lodge.

WM—Brother Senior Warden. where is your place in the Lodge?

SW—In the West.

WM—What is your duty there?

SW—As the Sun sets in the West to close the glorious day, so the Senior Warden stands in the West to close the Lodge, at the will and pleasure of the Worshipful Master.

WM—Let the Wardens declare to the Brethren, that it is my will and pleasure, that the Lodge do now close.

SW—Brethren, it is the will and pleasure of the Worshipful Master that the Lodge do now close.

JW—Brethren, it is the will and pleasure of the Worshipful Master that the Lodge do now close.

Whilst the Wardens are declaring 'the will and pleasure of the Worshipful Master,' the Deacons, the Director of ceremonies, and the Chaplain assemble at the Altar in the same positions as at the Opening, except that the Deacons will place their Wands in the coping position. When this is done, the Worshipful Master proceeds.

WM—Accordingly, Brethren, in the Name of The Great Architect of the Universe, I declare the Lodge to be closed, and to remain closed, until our next Stated Communication, except in case or cases of emergency of which each Brother entitled thereto shall receive due notice by Summons.

At the words 'I declare the Lodge to be now closed,' the Deacons will bring down the Wands to their right sides, the Director of Ceremonies will disarrange the Three Great Lights, an the Wardens will reverse their Pillars.

27

CHAPLAIN—May the blessing of Heaven rest upon us, and all regular Masons; may Brotherly-love prevail, and every moral and social virtue cement and unite us. So mote it be.

WM—⚬ ⚬ ⚬
SW—⚬ ⚬ ⚬
JW—⚬ ⚬ ⚬
IG—⚬ ⚬ ⚬
TYLER—⚬ ⚬ ⚬

All Brethren (except the Deacons) salute the Worshipful Master. A Hymn may also be sung at this time.

CALLING UP FROM E.A. TO F.C.

WM—Brother Secretary, what is the next business?

SECY—Worshipful Master, to call up the Lodge.

WM—Brethren, as I am about to call up the Lodge to the Second or Fellowcraft Degree; any Brother who has not yet received that Degree must now retire.

All Entered Apprentices present now rise, proceed to the centre of the Lodge Room, face the Worshipful Master and salute him. The Inner Guard knocks and, the Tyler having answered, opens the door. The Entered Apprentices retire from the Lodge Room and the door is again closed.

WM— ⚊⚊ Rise Brethren, and assist me to call up the Lodge.

WM—⚊⚊ — ⚊⚊⚊⚊

SW—⚊⚊ — ⚊⚊⚊⚊

JW—⚊⚊ — ⚊⚊⚊⚊

WM—Brother Junior Warden, what is the first care of a Master in calling up the Lodge?

JW—To see that the Lodge is tyled.

WM—See that duty performed.

JW—Brother Inner Guard, see that the Lodge is tyled.

IG—⚊⚊ — ⚊⚊⚊⚊

TYLER—⚊⚊ — ⚊⚊⚊⚊

IG—*Opens the door.*

TYLER—Brother Inner Guard, the Lodge is tyled.

IG—(*Closes the door*) Brother Junior Warden, the Lodge is tyled.

JW—Worshipful Master, the Lodge is tyled.

WM—Brother Senior Warden, what next demands our care?

SW—To see that each Brother present is in that Degree of Freemasonry to which the Lodge is about to be called up.

WM—How is that to be ascertained?

SW—By giving a Pass Word and exhibiting a Sign or by personal vouching.

WM—Can you personally vouch all present? (*)[5]

SW—I cannot.

WM—Call the Deacons together, see that they are properly instructed; direct them to receive the Pass Word from each Brother present, and report same to me.

SW—Let the Deacons approach.

The Deacons go to the Senior Warden in exactly the same manner as in the Opening Ceremony. The Senior Deacon will hand his Wand to the Junior Deacon so that he, the Senior Deacon, may give the Pass Grip and Pass Word to the Senior Warden. The Senior Deacon then takes both Wands from the Junior Deacon so that the Junior Deacon may give the Senior Warden the Pass Grip and Pass Word. The Junior Deacon then takes back his Wand. The Deacons proceed to take up the Pass Word and Pass Grip as in the Opening of the Lodge, and finally give the Pass Word and Pass Grip to the Worshipful Master, when the Deacons return to their respective position.

WM—Brethren, I have received the Pass Word.

WM—Brother Senior Warden, direct the Brethren to stand to order in that Degree of Freemasonry to which the Lodge is about to be called up.

SW—Brethren, it is the will and pleasure of the Worshipful Master that you do stand to order in that Degree of Freemasonry to which the Lodge is about to be called up.

All the Brethren now sand 'to Order.' The Senior Warden satisfies himself that all are giving the Sign correctly and he, standing to Order, says:—

---

[5]If the Senior Warden CAN personally vouch all present (which he must be able to do without assistance) the Ceremony between the two asterisks (*) is omitted. The Senior Warden responds "I can," and the Worshipful Master proceeds, "Let the Wardens declare to the Brethren..." *etc.*

SW—Worshipful Master, the Brethren have given me this Sign.

WM—Which I acknowledge to be correct, and thus ratify it. (*)

WM—Let the Wardens declare to the Brethren that it is my will and pleasure that the Lodge do now resume Labour.

SW—Brethren, it is the will and pleasure of the Worshipful Master that the Lodge do now resume Labour.

JW—Brethren, it is the will and pleasure of the Worshipful Master that the Lodge do now resume Labour.

WM—Accordingly, Brethren, in the Name of the Most High God, The Great Geometrician of the Universe, I declare the Lodge to be now at Labour on this, the Second or Fellowcrafts Degree, for the transaction of all such business as may be regularly brought before it; your Pass Word being —, and this — (*making the sign*) your True Guard and Sign.

WM— -◄ — ◄ ◄

SW— -◄ — ◄ ◄

JW— -◄ — ◄ ◄

IG— -◄ — ◄ ◄

TYLER— -◄ — ◄ ◄

BRN—*Salute and sit down.*

While the Wardens are declaring 'the will and pleasure of the Worshipful Master,' the Director of Ceremonies ALONE goes before the Altar, and when the Worshipful Master declares 'the Lodge to be now at Labour' on the Fellowcraft Degree, the Director of Ceremonies will arrange the Three Great Lights accordingly.

The business of the Lodge, if any, on this Degree now proceeds.

SECOND DEGREE
OR
CEREMONY OF PASSING

It is recommended that the Director of Ceremonies should retire from the Lodge room, and assist in the Preparation of the Candidate. When the Candidate is ready the usual Knocks are given by the Tyler.

N.B.—In preparing the Candidate the Cable Tow is placed TWO times around the neck.

IG—Worshipful Master, there is an alarm at the Candidate's Porch.

[If there is not a special door for Candidates, the Inner Guard will use the following:—

IG—Worshipful Master, there is an alarm at the door of the Porch.]

WM—Ascertain the cause thereof.

Inner Guard knocks on door, waits until answered by the Knocks from without. Inner Guard opens door, receives the information from the Tyler, and closes the door.

IG—Brother —, who has served his just and lawful time as an Entered Apprentice, now seeks to be passed to the Degree of Fellowcraft.

WM—How does he hope to obtain so great an honour?

Inner Guard Knocks on the door, waits until answered by the knocks from without. Inner Guard opens the door, receives the information from the Tyler and closes the door.

IG—By the benefit of a Pass Word which he has not yet received, but which the Tyler will give for him, by permission of the Worshipful Master.

WM—Admit him, on receiving the Word from the Tyler.

Inner Guard Knocks on the door, waits until answered by the knocks from without. Inner Guard opens the door, receives the Word and Grip from the Tyler and admits the Candidate.

The Conductor leads the Candidate to the Northwest Corner, that is, to the left of the Senior Warden, and halts the Candidate in front of a kneeling cushion. By this time the Deacons will be in position, the Senior Deacon to the left of the Candidate, and the Junior Deacon to the right. The Chaplain will have the appropriate Prayer ready.

COND.—Brother, on being admitted to receive the Degree of Entered Apprentice you were received as a stranger in darkness, with a Halter round your neck, and a hostile weapon pointed at your naked and defenseless breast. The Masonic significance of these various points have been duly explained to you.

We now receive you as a Brother on the angle of a Square, thereby enjoining you to see that all your dealings with your fellow men are strictly honourable, straightforward, and on the Square.

COND.—(*turning toward Worshipful Master*) Worshipful Master, the Candidate has been received according to Ancient Custom.

WM—Let him kneel, and receive the benefit of prayer.

Excepting the Candidate, all the Brethren rise. Chaplain reads the prayer. Candidate then rises, and is led by the Conductor three times round the Lodge Room, the Deacons walking in front. First time around, when passing before the Worshipful Master, the Candidate and Conductor will halt and salute the Worshipful Master with the Entered Apprentice Sign. Having saluted the Worshipful Master, the Candidate passes in front of the Junior Warden, but behind the Senior Warden. On the second time around, following the same procedure, the Candidate is halted at the right of the Senior Warden. The Conductor takes the Candidate's Right Hand, and with it gives the knocks of the Degree on the Right Shoulder of the Senior Warden, who says:—

SW—Who comes here?

COND.—Brother —, who has served his just and lawful time as an Entered Apprentice, now seeks to be passed to the Degree of Fellowcraft.

SW—How does he hope to obtain so great an honour?

COND.—By the benefit of a Pass Word which he has not yet received, but which I will give for him, by permission of the Worshipful Master.

Conductor moves the Candidate back a few paces and approaches the Senior Warden, to whom he gives the Pass Word and Pass Grip of a Fellowcraft.

SW—Let him pass.

The Pedestal or Table of the Senior Warden in now moved forward and both the Candidate and Conductor pass between the Chair and the Pedestal of the Senior Warden. The Deacons should be in position to lead the procession. The Candidate is halted before the Worshipful Master where both he and the Conductor salute as Entered Apprentices. The Deacons stand at both sides of the Conductor and Candidate; the Senior Deacon to the left, the Junior Deacon to the right.

COND.—Worshipful Master, I present to you our Brother Entered Apprentice —, who seeks to be passed to the Degree of Fellowcraft. He has duly passed the Western Gate.

WM—Take him to the Senior Warden, and crave his fraternal assistance in having the Candidate placed in the proper position in order to take the Obligation peculiar to this Degree.

The Deacons precede the Conductor and the Candidate before the Senior Warden, about two paces from the Altar; they face the Senior Warden. The Deacons stand a little to the side; the Senior Deacon to the South side, the Junior Deacon to the North side.

COND.—Brother Senior Warden, by direction of the Worshipful Master, I present to you our Brother Entered Apprentice, who seeks to be passed to the Degree of Fellowcraft; and I crave your fraternal assistance in having him placed in the proper position to take the Obligation peculiar to this Degree.

SW—Let the Candidate stand erect, and face the East.

The Conductor turns the Candidate right, so that he faces the Altar. Deacons also turn and face the East.

SW—Let him advance and salute as an Entered Apprentice. (*Done.*)

Let him take one step forward with the Right Foot, placing the heel of the Left Foot in the Hollow of the Right Foot, forming a Square. (*Pause until Candidate completes the step.*)

Let him kneel on the Right Knee on the second of a series of steps before the Altar, squaring the Left Leg. (*Done.*)

Let him place the Right Hand over the Volume of the Sacred Law and raise his Left Arm.

The Conductor assists the Candidate in these movements, showing him how to square the left arm. He directs the Junior Deacon to support the upraised arm with the interior angle of a Square and the Deacon's Wand. The Square is placed under the Candidate's elbow.

COND.—Worshipful Master, the Candidate is now in the proper position to take the Obligation.

WM—Brother —, as we are now about to communicate to you the secrets peculiar to this degree, we require you to take an Obligation of secrecy.

With regard to this Obligation, I give you my assurance that there is nothing in it at variance with your religious belief, political opinion, the allegiance you owe to your Sovereign or the Rulers of the State to which you belong. Nor is there anything in it hurtful to your feelings as a man of honour.

I further assure you that, with the exception of yourself, everyone here present has already taken this Obligation.

Having this assurance from me, are you now willing to take this Obligation, and by it become bound to us, as we are to one another?

Can.—I am.

OBLIGATION

I, — —, of my own free-will and accord, in the presence of the Most High God, the Great Geometrician of the Universe, and of this worthy, worshipful and warranted Lodge of Ancient, Free and Accepted Masons, regularly constituted, properly assembled and duly dedicated in His Most Holy Name, do hereby—*Conductor lightly raises the Candidate's right hand*—and hereon—*Conductor replaces the Candidate's right hand*—solemnly and sincerely promise, vow and declare that I will ever hele, conceal, and never will reveal unlawfully, aught of the hidden points, secrets, or mysteries of, or belonging to this, the Second or Fellowcraft Degree of Freemasonry which have been heretofore, shall now, or may hereafter become known to me in any way whatsoever.

I will not communicate, divulge or discover these secrets to anyone in the whole world except to him or to them to whom the same do surely, justly and of right belong, that is to say, in the body of a Lodge of Freemasons just, perfect and regular and at labour on the Second or Fellowcraft Degree, or to a well-known Brother Fellowcraft, or to one who is duly vouched to me at the mouth of a well-known Brother Fellowcraft, or to one whom after due trial and strict examination I shall find to be lawfully entitled to the same.

I will answer all regular Signs and summonses; Signs thrown to me from the hand of a well-known Brother of the Craft and summonses reaching me from a regular Lodge of Ancient Craft Masons, provided I be not prevented by sickness, imprisonment or by the pressure of public or private duty, and that I be within two miles of the place where summoned to attend.

I promise, vow and declare that I will help, relieve and assist poor and necessitous Fellowcrafts, they making application to me as such, and I having satisfied myself that they are fit and worthy of such relief; provided that the giving of such relief be not prejudicial to my own interests or to those of my familiar or close personal friends.

All these points I solemnly promise, vow and declare that I will observe without any evasion, equivocation or mental reservation whatsoever, bearing in mind the ancient penalty of having the l.b.t.o. and h. pl. from thence and thrown as a p. to the birds of the air, and binding myself under the real penalty of being deservedly branded as a wretch, base, faithless and unworthy to be received among men of honour, should I knowingly or willfully violate in letter or spirit this my most solemn, sincere and voluntary Obligation as an Fellowcraft Freemason.

WM—You will now ratify the Obligation you have just taken by kissing the Volume of the Sacred Law, which lies between your hands or in any other manner equally binding on your conscience.

Candidate ratifies.

COND.—As your previous degree, so once again in this degree we are known to each other by Sound, by Touch and by Sight. In Sound, by Knocks and Words; in Touch, by grips; and by Sight, by certain regular Signs.

The Knocks of the Degree are given thus: ▬▬◄ — ▬◄ ▬◄. Should you, at any time, find yourself outside the closed door of a Masonic Lodge, and hear these Knocks given on the door, you will understand that within there is a Lodge at Labour on this, the Degree of Fellowcraft.

To gain admission to the Lodge working on this Degree you would have to possess a 'Pass Word,' which is accompanied by a certain Pass Grip, or handshake. The Pass Word is revealed in a certain passage of

Scripture which refers to an incident in the history of the Israelites when they were ruled by Judges.

At this particular time Jephthah was Judge over Israel and had succeeded in subduing the turbulent Ammonites. The Ephraimites were jealous of Jephthah's victory, and annoyed that they were not called to take part in the fight against the Ammonites and so share in the spoils of war. They angered Jephthah so greatly that he determined to punish them. You will now hear the first six verses of the 12th Chapter of Judges read, which will tell you how Jephthah punished the Ephraimites, and also reveal the word which is used as the Pass Word for this Degree.

COND. (*or* **CHAPLAIN**)—'And the men of Ephraim gathered themselves together, and went northward, and said unto Jephthah, Wherefore passedst thou over to fight against the children of Ammon, and didst not call us to go with thee? we will burn thine house upon thee with fire.

And Jephthah said unto them, I and my people were at great strife with the children of Ammon; and when I called you, ye delivered me not out of their hands.

And when I saw that ye delivered me not, I put my life in my hands, and passed over against the children of Ammon, and the LORD delivered them into my hand: wherefore then are ye come up unto me this day, to fight against me?

Then Jephthah gathered together all the men of Gilead, and fought with Ephraim: and the men of Gilead smote Ephraim, because they said, Ye Gileadites are fugitives of Ephraim among the Ephraimites, and among the Manassites.

And the Gileadites took the passages of Jordan before the Ephraimites: and it was so that when those Ephraimites which were escaped said, Let me go over; that the men of Gilead said unto him, Art thou an Ephraimite? If he said, Nay;

Then said they unto him, Say now Shibboleth: and he said Sibboleth: for he could not frame to pronounce it right. Then they took him, and slew him at the passages of Jordan: and there fell at that time of the Ephraimites forty and two thousand.'

The Conductor explains the accompanying Grip, impressing the fact that the Word and Grip must be given in connection with each other.

COND.—Thus, to gain admission to a Lodge at Labour on this, the Degree of Fellowcraft, after the knocks of the Degree have been given by the Tyler and the door is opened, you would give this Pass Word and Pass Grip, covered with the left hand, to the Inner Guard, who would permit you to enter.

At a certain part of the Ceremony of Calling Up the Lodge from the Degree of Fellowcraft, the Deacons will be instructed to take the Pass Word from each Brother present, and when one of the Deacons comes to you, you would give him this Pass Word and Pass Grip, covered with the left hand, when he will be satisfied that you are qualified to remain in the room.

The Secret Word of this degree is —. It is also accompanied by a Grip given thus: (*demonstrating*) and covered. In giving this Word under examination you will use the same caution as impressed upon you in your previous degree. The Word and Grip are not used ordinarily in our ceremonies, but may be asked from you if proving yourself as a Brother Fellowcraft.

At the door of the Porch of the Great Temple of King Solomon there were placed two Pillars of Brass, one at the left an the other at the right side of the entrance. That on the left was called BOAZ, and that on the right, JACHIN. In the Hebrew tongue BOAZ means, 'In strength,' and JACHIN, 'To establish.' [Thus, by the combined words may be interpreted, 'I, the Lord, will establish this my house in strength.']⁶

The Pillars were placed there also to remind the people of Israel of the wonderful protection of the Almighty who led their forefathers through the wilderness with a Pillar of Cloud by day and of Fire by night. With this

---

⁶This sentence is sometimes omitted.

Secret Word and Grip I assist you to rise from the kneeling position, as a duly obligated Fellowcraft Freemason.

The Signs of the Degree are the Due Guard, and the True Guard or Salute. When you advanced to the Altar to take the Obligation you advanced first as an Entered Apprentice. You then took a step forward with the right foot and placed the heel of the left foot in the hollow of the right foot forming a square.

Now, place your feet in that position and your hands as when taking the Obligation. (*Conductor goes through the movement, at the same time directing the Candidate to repeat same.*) You are now standing with the Sign of the Due Guard of the degree. The Sign of the Due Guard is not used in the ceremonies under the Constitution of Ireland, but it is used elsewhere under other Masonic governments. You may now drop your hands.

Once again, paying attention to the position of your feet (*Conductor places his own feet in position and directs Candidate to do likewise.*) and calling to mind the ancient penalty referred to in the Obligation of this degree you give the Salute or True Guard as follows: (*Conductor explains and directs the Candidate to follow the movements*). Should you at any time address the Worshipful Master, when the Lodge should be at Labour on the Master Mason Degree, you would give him this Salute when you rise to speak or, when crossing the floor of the Lodge room, you would halt when passing the Worshipful Master, face him and salute as instructed, and then proceed across the room.

At a certain part of the Ceremony of 'Calling Up' the Lodge, the Brethren will be instructed to stand to Order in that Degree on which the Lodge is about to be called up. You would give the first part of the salute thus: (*demonstrating*); wait until it is ratified by the Worshipful Master; then complete the Sign thus: (*demonstrating*).

Referring to the Obligation, it is composed of three clauses, which are Secrecy, Obedience and Charity. You will note that the name of the Deity is changed, and in this degree the Most High God is referred to as 'The Great Geometrician of the Universe.'

You will be careful to preserve the secrets of this degree, and not communicate them, except to those lawfully entitled thereto, as set out in the four exceptions stated. When being vouched, or vouching others, you will see that you are vouched Brother Fellowcrafts before entering into any conversation concerning this degree.

As regards satisfying yourself by examination of an unknown person, we would ask you to wait a little longer before you attempt such an experiment, so that you may learn more of our teaching, and in due time receive instruction as to the proper method of an examination.

The second clause, of Obedience, impresses on you the necessity of attending the meetings and observing the duties of your Lodge. You have promised to answer all regular Signs and Summonses. We believe that in years gone by it was the custom of the Master, or some other Brother deputed by him, to visit personally the members of the particular Lodge, giving notice of a meeting about to be held, and also giving a certain Sign. The Brethren were expected to answer this Summons and Sign by their attendance at the Lodge meeting. In these days it is customary to send notices of meetings by post which are just as binding on you as the giving of the Sign to our ancient Brethren.

Freemasonry does not ask or expect what may be an impossibility, and makes certain exceptions. You may be prevented from attending by sickness or imprisonment, or again by the pressure of public or private duty. But, we do ask you to endeavor to give the Lodge meetings preference if you may be called on for some public or private engagement at the time of your Lodge meeting. There is a further exception mentioned in the Obligation, which is called the 'Traveling Distance' or Masonic 'Cable Tow,' stating 'provided I be within two miles of the place where summoned to attend.' As regards that exception we ask you not to take it too literally, nor make such a short distance an excuse for your absence from Lodge. This provision was framed when traveling was not so easy or so safe as it is today, but as it is handed down to us in the Obligation, so we hand it on to you, trusting to your discretion as to how you make use of it.

In the third clause, of Charity, you have promised to help, relieve, and assist poor and necessitous Fellowcrafts, they making application to you as such. Before you grant any such request, you will not that you are expected to satisfy yourself that the Brother making the request is a fit and worthy object of relief, and further, you are protected by the provision made in the Obligation which releases you from giving the required assistance should it be likely to prove prejudicial to your own interests, or those of your family or close personal friends.

THE DEMAND

As a test of your sincerity I now ask you, can you give me anything to assist the well-serving case of a destitute Brother? Can you place any contribution of money on this Square?

Conductor holds out Square to the Candidate and waits until the Candidate gives his reply; usually, that he has been temporarily deprived of his money.

COND.—Brother, this is not done to cause you embarrassment, but for certain reasons. Firstly, to prove to the assembled Brethren that you are properly prepared, because if you were able to produce even the smallest coin or article of value, the conferring of this degree would have proved irregular. Secondly, to remind you in years to come that at one time in your life you stood actually penniless in the midst of plenty. Thirdly, to impress on you to be ever ready to listen to the requests of necessitous Brethren, and make every effort to assist them, guided by the provisions made as to the giving of relief.

You have promised to observe this Obligation by bearing in mind the ancient penalty, and binding yourself under the real penalty of being deservedly branded as a wretch, base, faithless, and unworthy to be received among men of honour should you ever violate this solemn Obligation.

WORKING TOOLS

As in the former degree, so in this we use certain implements of the Operative Mason which teach us moral lessons, and known to us as the Working Tools of the degree. These are the Square, the Level, and the Plumb-Rule.

The Square is an angle of 90 degrees, or the fourth part of a circle. It is an important implement in the hands of the Operative Masons, for by it they are enabled to correct errors of the eye, and adjust with precision the edges, angles and sides of the work they are engaged upon. The truest joints are thus constructed, and stones fitted to fill, with accuracy, their destined positions. To the Speculative Mason the Square is an emblem or morality, as by the application of the Square the stone is tried and proved, so by the principles of Morality each action of human life is judged.

The Level is an implement used for testing horizontals, and to the Speculative Mason and emblem of Equality. Not that social equality, which leveling all distinction of rank would tend to beget confusion and anarchy, but that of the Fraternal equality which should always be found in the Lodge.

It teaches us that in sight of God, all men are equal, subject to the same infirmities, hastening to the same goal, and preparing to be judged by the same immutable laws. and reminds us of that vast level of time on which all men are traveling to its limit in Eternity.

The Plumb-Rule is an implement used for testing perpendiculars, and to the Speculative Mason and emblem of rectitude of conduct.

As a building is not erected on a perpendicular line, but leaning one way or the other becomes insecure and must eventually fall, so he whose life is not supported by an upright course of conduct cannot long sustain a worthy reputation, and must soon sink beneath the estimation of every good and virtuous man.

The Candidate is now brought before the Worshipful Master and invested with the appropriate Apron. He is then placed in the Northeast corner of the Lodge Room while the Charge is read to him.

CHARGE TO THE FELLOWCRAFT MASON

Brother, as you have now been passed to the Second Degree of Freemasonry, it becomes my duty to remind you of the responsibilities which, by your entrance into our Society, you have bound yourself to discharge, and of the necessity for a conscientious endeavour to fulfill your voluntary obligations. Your experience in the previous degree will have given you an insight into our tenet; and in your new character it is expected that you will not only assent to the principles of the Craft, but steadily persevere in their practice.

The First Degree is intended to enforce the duties of Fidelity, Candour and Discretion, and thereby to safeguard the noblest principles which can adorn the human mind. The Second Degree extends the plan, and develops a comprehensive system of benevolence. The responsibilities of our new position require you to be particularly attentive to your behaviour at our assemblies. You are never to neglect the duty of being present, when regularly summoned at our meetings, subject only to the exception already explained to you. You are to help the weak, to relieve the distressed and to assist the struggling and industrious among your fellows in the Craft, to the utmost of your power and ability.

As a craftsman, in our private assemblies, you are entitled to offer your opinion on such subjects as are regularly introduced under the superintendence of the Master, whose duty it is to guard our Landmarks from encroachment. Thus, you may improve your intellectual powers, qualify yourself to be a useful member of our Society, and eventually become a skillful Craftsman, by constantly striving to excel is which is good and great.

The Candidate is now seated in the Northeast corner and saluted.

CALLING DOWN FROM AN
F.C. TO E.A.

WM—Brother Secretary, have you any further business for transaction on this degree?

SECY—Worshipful Master, there is no further business for consideration.

WM—⚫ Rise, Brethren, and assist me to call down the Lodge.

WM—⚫ ⚫ ⚫

SW—⚫ ⚫ ⚫

JW—⚫ ⚫ ⚫

WM—Brother Junior Warden, what is the first care of a Master in calling down the Lodge?

WM—See that duty performed.

JW—Brother Inner Guard, see that the Lodge is tyled.

IG—⚫ ⚫ ⚫

TYLER—⚫ ⚫ ⚫

IG—*Opens the door*.

Tyler—Brother Inner Guard, the Lodge is tyled.

IG—(*Closes the door*) Brother Junior Warden, the Lodge is tyled.

JW—Worshipful Master, the Lodge is tyled.

WM—Let the Wardens declare to the Brethren that it is my will and pleasure that the Lodge do now resume Labour.

SW—Brethren, it is the will and pleasure of the Worshipful Master that the Lodge do now resume Labour.

JW—Brethren, it is the will and pleasure of the Worshipful Master that the Lodge do now resume Labour.

WM—Accordingly, Brethren, in the Name of the Most High God, The Great Architect of the Universe, I declare the Lodge to be now at Labour on the First or Entered Apprentice Degree of Freemasonry, for the transaction of all such business as may be regularly brought before it; your Entrance Pass being 'By the help of God, and the tongue of good report,' and this — (*making the sign*) your True Guard and Sign.

WM—⚫ ⚫ ⚫

45

WM — ⚊🔨 ⚊🔨 ⚊🔨

SW — ⚊🔨 ⚊🔨 ⚊🔨

JW — ⚊🔨 ⚊🔨 ⚊🔨

IG — ⚊🔨 ⚊🔨 ⚊🔨

TYLER — ⚊🔨 ⚊🔨 ⚊🔨

BRN—*Salute and sit down.*

While the Wardens are declaring 'the will and pleasure of the Worshipful Master,' the Director of Ceremonies ALONE goes before the Altar, and when the Worshipful Master declares 'the Lodge to be now at Labour' on the Fellowcraft Degree, the Director of Ceremonies will arrange the Three Great Lights accordingly.

CALLING UP FROM F.C. TO M.M.

WM—Brother Secretary, what is the next business?

SECY—Worshipful Master, to call up the Lodge.

WM—Brethren, as I am about to call up the Lodge to the Third or Sublime Degree of Master Mason; any Brother who has not yet received that Degree must now retire.

All Fellowcrafts present now rise, proceed to the centre of the Lodge Room, face the Worshipful Master and salute him. The Inner Guard knocks and, the Tyler having answered, opens the door. The Fellowcrafts retire from the Lodge Room and the door is again closed.

WM—▬▬▬ Rise Brethren, and assist me to call up the Lodge.

WM—▬▬ ▬▬ — ▬▬

SW—▬▬ ▬▬ — ▬▬

JW—▬▬ ▬▬ — ▬▬

WM—Brother Junior Warden, what is the first care of a Master in calling up the Lodge?

JW—To see that the Lodge is tyled.

WM—See that duty performed.

JW—Brother Inner Guard, see that the Lodge is tyled.

IG—▬▬ ▬▬ — ▬▬

TYLER—▬▬ ▬▬ — ▬▬

IG—*Opens the door.*

TYLER—Brother Inner Guard, the Lodge is tyled.

IG—(*Closes the door*) Brother Junior Warden, the Lodge is tyled.

JW—Worshipful Master, the Lodge is tyled.

WM—Brother Senior Warden, what next demands our care?

SW—To see that each Brother present is in that Degree of Freemasonry to which the Lodge is about to be called up.

WM—How is that to be ascertained?

SW—By giving a Pass Word and exhibiting a Sign or by personal vouching.

SW—By giving a Pass Word and exhibiting a Sign or by personal vouching.

WM—Can you personally vouch all present? (*)[7]

SW—I cannot.

WM—Call the Deacons together, see that they are properly instructed; direct them to receive the Pass Word from each Brother present, and report same to me.

SW—Let the Deacons approach.

The Deacons go to the Senior Warden in exactly the same manner as in the Opening Ceremony. The Senior Deacon will hand his Wand to the Junior Deacon so that he, the Senior Deacon, may give the Pass Grip and Pass Word to the Senior Warden. The Senior Deacon then takes both Wands from the Junior Deacon so that the Junior Deacon may give the Senior Warden the Pass Grip and Pass Word. The Junior Deacon then takes back his Wand. The Deacons proceed to take up the Pass Word and Pass Grip as in the Opening of the Lodge, and finally give the Pass Word and Pass Grip to the Worshipful Master, when the Deacons return to their respective position.

WM—Brethren, I have received the Pass Word.

WM—Brother Senior Warden, direct the Brethren to stand to order in that Degree of Freemasonry to which the Lodge is about to be called up.

SW—Brethren, it is the will and pleasure of the Worshipful Master that you do stand to order in that Degree of Freemasonry to which the Lodge is about to be called up.

All the Brethren now sand 'to Order.' The Senior Warden satisfies himself that all are giving the Sign correctly and he, standing to Order, says:—

---

[7] As in the preceding degree, if the Senior Warden CAN personally vouch all present (which he must be able to do without assistance) the Ceremony between the two asterisks (*) is omitted. The Senior Warden responds "I can," and the Worshipful Master proceeds, "Let the Wardens declare to the Brethren..." *etc.*

SW—Worshipful Master, the Brethren have given me this Sign.

WM—Which I acknowledge to be correct, and thus ratify it. (*)

WM—Let the Wardens declare to the Brethren that it is my will and pleasure that the Lodge do now resume Labour.

SW—Brethren, it is the will and pleasure of the Worshipful Master that the Lodge do now resume Labour.

JW—Brethren, it is the will and pleasure of the Worshipful Master that the Lodge do now resume Labour.

WM—Accordingly, Brethren, in the Name of the Most High God, The Great God of the Universe, I declare the Lodge to be now at Labour on this, the Third or Sublime Degree of Master Mason, for the transaction of all such business as may be regularly brought before it; your Pass Word being —, and this — (*making the sign*) your True Guard and Sign.

WM—⊶⊶ – ⊶

SW—⊶⊶ – ⊶

JW—⊶⊶ – ⊶

IG—⊶⊶ – ⊶

TYLER—⊶⊶ – ⊶

BRN—*Salute and sit down.*

While the Wardens are declaring 'the will and pleasure of the Worshipful Master,' the Director of Ceremonies ALONE goes before the Altar, and when the Worshipful Master declares 'the Lodge to be now at Labour' on the Fellowcraft Degree, the Director of Ceremonies will arrange the Three Great Lights accordingly.

The business of the Lodge, if any, on this Degree now proceeds.

THIRD DEGREE
OR
CEREMONY OF RAISING

It is recommended that the Director of Ceremonies should retire from the Lodge room, and assist in the Preparation of the Candidate. When the Candidate is ready the usual Knocks are given by the Tyler.

N.B.—In preparing the Candidate the Cable Tow is placed ONE times around the neck.

IG—Worshipful Master, there is an alarm at the Candidate's Porch.

[If there is not a special door for Candidates, the Inner Guard will use the following:—

IG—Worshipful Master, there is an alarm at the door of the Porch.]

WM—Ascertain the cause thereof.

Inner Guard knocks on door, waits until answered by the Knocks from without. Inner Guard opens door, receives the information from the Tyler, and closes the door.

IG—Brother —, who has served his just and lawful time as an Entered Apprentice, and has wrought some time as a Fellowcraft, now seeks to be raised to the Sublime Degree of Master Mason.

WM—How does he hope to obtain so great an honour?

Inner Guard Knocks on the door, waits until answered by the knocks from without. Inner Guard opens the door, receives the information from the Tyler and closes the door.

IG—By the benefit of a Pass Word which he has not yet received, but which the Tyler will give for him, by permission of the Worshipful Master.

WM—Admit him, on receiving the Word from the Tyler.

WM—Admit him, on receiving the Word from the Tyler.

Inner Guard Knocks on the door, waits until answered by the knocks from without. Inner Guard opens the door, receives the Word and Grip from the Tyler and admits the Candidate.

The Conductor leads the Candidate to the Northwest Corner, that is, to the left of the Senior Warden, and halts the Candidate in front of a kneeling cushion. By this time the Deacons will be in position, the Senior Deacon to the left of the Candidate, and the Junior Deacon to the right. The Chaplain will have the appropriate Prayer ready.

COND.—Brother, on being admitted to receive the degree of Entered Apprentice you were received as a stranger in darkness, with a Halter round your neck, and a hostile weapon pointed at your naked and defenseless breast. On being admitted to receive the degree of Fellowcraft you were received as a Brother in the Light on the angle of the Square. The Masonic significance of these various points have been duly explained to you.

We now receive you on the extended Compasses, and as between these two points lie the most vital parts of your body, as the most vital secrets of Ancient Craft Masonry are comprehended in this, the Third or Sublime Degree of Master Mason.

COND.—(*turning toward Worshipful Master*) Worshipful Master, the Candidate has been received in accordance with Ancient Custom.

WM—Let him kneel, and receive the benefit of prayer.

Excepting the Candidate, all the Brethren rise. Chaplain reads the prayer. Candidate then rises, and is led by the Conductor three times round the Lodge Room, the Deacons walking in front. Each time around, when passing before the Worshipful Master, the Candidate and Conductor will halt and salute the Worshipful Master with the Fellowcrafts Sign. On coming before the Worshipful Master for the third time, the Deacons halt, one at each side of the Dais. The

Conductor leads the Candidate up to the Worshipful Master, and with the Candidate's right hand gives the Knocks of the Degree of the right shoulder of the Worshipful Master.

WM—Who comes here?

COND.—Brother —, who has served his just and lawful time as an Entered Apprentice, and has wrought some time as a Fellowcraft, now seeks to be raised to the Sublime Degree of Master Mason.

WM—How does he hope to obtain so great an honour?

COND.—By the benefit of a Pass Word which he has not yet received, but which I will give for him, by your permission.

Conductor leads Candidate down from the Dais, or if no Dais is used, a few paces back. Conductor then steps forward again and gives the Worshipful Master the Pass Word and Pass Grip.

WM—Take him to the Senior Warden, and crave his fraternal assistance in having the Candidate placed in the proper position in order to take the Obligation peculiar to this Degree.

The Deacons precede the Conductor and the Candidate before the Senior Warden, about three paces from the Altar; they face the Senior Warden. The Deacons stand a little to the side; the Senior Deacon to the South side, the Junior Deacon to the North side.

COND.—Brother Senior Warden, by direction of the Worshipful Master, I present to you our Brother Fellowcraft, who seeks to be raised to the Sublime Degree of Master Mason; and I crave your fraternal assistance in having him placed in the proper position to take the Obligation peculiar to this Degree.

SW—Let the Candidate stand erect, and face the East.

The Conductor turns the Candidate right, so that he faces the Altar. Deacons also turn and face the East.

SW—Let him advance and salute as an Entered Apprentice. (*Done.*)

Let him advance and salute as a Fellowcraft. (*Done.*)

Let him take one step forward with the left foot, placing the heel of the right foot to the heel of the left foot, forming a Square with the feet. (*Pause until Candidate completes the step.*)

Let him kneel on the third of a series of steps on both knees, placing both hands on the Volume of the Sacred Law.

The Conductor assists the Candidate in these movements.

COND.—Worshipful Master, the Candidate is now in the proper position to take the Obligation.

WM—Brother —, as we are now about to communicate to you the secrets peculiar to this degree, we require you to take an Obligation of secrecy.

With regard to this Obligation, I give you my assurance that there is nothing in it at variance with your religious belief, political opinion, the allegiance you owe to your Sovereign or the Rulers of the State to which you belong. Nor is there anything in it hurtful to your feelings as a man of honour.

I further assure you that, with the exception of yourself, everyone here present has already taken this Obligation.

Having this assurance from me, are you now willing to take this Obligation, and by it become bound to us, as we are to one another?

Can.—I am.

OBLIGATION

I, — —, of my own free-will and accord, in the presence of the Most High God, the Great God of the Universe, and of this worthy, worshipful and warranted Lodge of Ancient, Free and Accepted Masons, regularly constituted, properly assembled and duly dedicated in His Most Holy Name, do hereby—*Conductor lightly raises the Candidate's right hand*—and hereon—*Conductor replaces the Candidate's right hand*—solemnly and sincerely promise, vow and declare that I will ever hele, conceal, and never will reveal unlawfully, aught of the hidden points, secrets, or mysteries of, or belonging to this, the Third or Sublime Degree of Ancient Craft Masonry, which have been heretofore, shall now, or may hereafter become known to me in any way whatsoever.

I will not communicate, divulge or discover these secrets to anyone in the whole world except to him or to them to whom the same do surely, justly and of right belong, that is to say, in the body of a Lodge of Freemasons just, perfect and regular and at labour on the Master Masons Degree, or to a well-known Brother Master Mason, or to one who is duly vouched to me at the mouth of a well-known Brother Fellowcraft, or to one whom after due trial and strict examination I shall find to be lawfully entitled to the same.

I will answer all regular Signs and summonses; Signs thrown to me from the hand of a well-known Brother Master Mason and summonses reaching me from a regular Lodge of Ancient Craft Masons, provided I be not prevented by sickness, imprisonment or by the pressure of public or private duty, and that I be within three miles of the place where summoned to attend.

I promise, vow and declare that I will help, relieve and assist poor and necessitous Master Masons, they making application to me as such, and I having satisfied myself that they are fit and worthy of such relief; provided that the giving of such relief be not prejudicial to my own interests or to those of my familiar or close personal friends.

I will not wrong or defraud my Brother Master Mason, nor suffer the same to be done by another if in my power to prevent it.

I will give my Brother Master Mason timely warning of impending danger, so that he may be prepared to go forth to meet it, or step aside and avoid it.

I will keep my Brother Master Mason's secret as inviolably as my own, provided it be duly communicated to me and by me accepted as such; murder, treason, and the like offenses against the laws of God and man being excepted, and left to my own free will and discretion.

I will guard the honour and protect the chastity of my Brother Master Mason's wife, sister, daughter or other near relative.

All these points I solemnly promise, vow and declare that I will observe without any evasion, equivocation or mental reservation whatsoever, bearing in mind the ancient penalty of having the b.sn. in tn. the b. taken thence, and with the b.b.t.a., and the a.s. to the f.w. of heaven, and binding myself under the real penalty of being deservedly branded as a wretch, base, faithless and unworthy to be received among men of honour, should I knowingly or willfully violate in letter or spirit, this my most solemn, sincere and voluntary Obligation as an Master Mason.

WM—You will now ratify the Obligation you have just taken by kissing the Volume of the Sacred Law, which lies between your hands or in any other manner equally binding on your conscience.

Candidate ratifies.

COND.—Once again in this degree we are known to each other by Sound, by Touch and by Sight. In Sound, by Knocks and Words; in Touch, by grips; and by Sight, by certain regular Signs.

The Knocks of the Degree are given thus: ━▮ ━▮ — ━▮. Should you, at any time, find yourself outside the closed door of a Masonic Lodge, and hear these Knocks given on the door, you will understand that within there is a Lodge at Labour on this, the Degree of Master Mason.

To gain admission to the Lodge it is necessary to be in possession of a Pass Word. The Pass Word of this degree is — —, and accompanied by a Pass Grip given thus: (*demonstrates*).

The knocks of this degree are given on the door by the Tyler, and when the door is opened, you would give this Pass Word and Pass Grip covered to the Inner Guard, who would permit you to enter.

At a certain part of the ceremony of calling up the Lodge from the degree of Fellowcraft to the degree of Master Mason, the Deacons will be instructed to take the Pass Word from each Brother present, and when one of the Deacons comes to you, you would give him this word and covered Pass Grip, when he will satisfied that you are well qualified to remain in the room.

With this Pass Word and Pass Grip I assist you to rise from the kneeling position, as a duly Obligated Master Mason.

The Signs of the degree are the Due Guard and the True Guard, or Salute.

When you advanced to the altar to take your Obligation you advanced first as an Entered Apprentice, symbolizing the first Step in Freemasonry. Again, advancing as a Fellowcraft, symbolizing the second Step in Freemasonry. Again advancing, you took a further step forward with the left foot, placing the heel of the right foot to the heel of the left foot, forming a Square with the feet, thus symbolizing the third step in Freemasonry.

Now, place your feet in that position and your hands as when taking the Obligation. (*Conductor goes through the movement, at the same time directing the Candidate to repeat same.*) You are now standing with the Sign of the Due Guard of the Degree. The Sign of the Due Guard is not used in the ceremonies under the Constitution of Ireland, but it is used elsewhere under other Masonic governments. You may now drop your hands.

Again paying attention to the position of your feet (*Conductor places his own feet in position and directs Candidate to do likewise.*) and calling to mind the ancient penalty referred to in the Obligation of this degree you give the Salute or True Guard as follows: (*Conductor explains and directs the Candidate to follow the movements*). Should you at any time address the Worshipful Master, when the Lodge should be at Labour on the Master Mason Degree, you would give him this Salute when you rise to speak or, when crossing the floor of the Lodge room, you would halt when passing the Worshipful Master, face him and salute as instructed, and then proceed across the room.

At a certain part of the Ceremony of 'Calling Up' the Lodge, the Brethren will be instructed to stand to Order in that Degree on which the Lodge is about to be called up. You would give the first part of the salute thus: (*demonstrating*); wait until it is ratified by the Worshipful Master; then complete the Sign thus: (*demonstrating*).

Referring to the Obligation, it is composed of seven clauses, thus symbolically binding us by a sevenfold tie. You will note that the name of the Deity is changed, and in this degree the Most High God is referred to as 'The Great God of the Universe.'

You will be careful to preserve the secrets of this degree, and not reveal the same unlawfully; and, when vouching or being vouched, you will see that all concerned are vouched Brother Master Masons before entering into any conversation concerning this degree.

The Obedience clause is similar to that of the Fellowcraft, except in this case the traveling distance is extended to three miles, and we expect you will not use even that limitation as an excuse for non-attendance in your Masonic duties.

The Charity clause is also similar in explanation as given in the previous degree, but you will hold a Brother Master Mason in a closer tie than a Brother of a lower degree.

The fourth clause is, of course, new to you, and may seem strange that as a man of honour your should be asked to promise that you will not wrong or defraud a Brother Master Mason. But, it is more especially to the latter part of the clause that we draw attention, that is, 'nor will you permit the same to be done by another, if in your power to prevent it.' Thus we are assured that the welfare of your Brother Master Mason is safely protected by you whether in his presence or his absence.

The fifth clause refers to the giving of timely warning of impending danger. In years gone past it was customary for Operative Masons to travel from town to town as required by the work they might be called on to perform. Traveling was no so safe in those far-off days as it may be today, and so Operative Masons, having had experience of the difficulties and perils on the their journey, might be following on the road. This is intended to remind us that it is our duty to warn our Brethren of anything we know which might be likely to hurt them. For instance, a Brother may be about to engage in some transaction connected with his business or profession of which you are aware, and of which you have information you believe is not known to him, to the effect that if he undertakes this engagement it will prove hurtful to his interests, you are bound to give him timely warning, so that being forewarned he may be prepared to go forth to meet it, or step aside and avoid it. If the advice is not taken, then you are absolved from blame, having fulfilled your Obligation.

The sixth clause refers to keeping secret information given you by a Brother Master Mason. You have promised that you will keep your Brother Master Mason's secret as inviolably as your own, provided it is duly communicated to you, and by your received as such. A duly communicated secret is one which is given to you and accepted by you Masonically, or on the Square. If a Brother Master Mason says to you, 'I want to tell you a secret'—well, you accept it and treat it as you would a secret from any ordinary acquaintance. But, if he says, 'I want to tell you something on the Square,' and you say, 'No, I do not wish to take the information in that way,' then there is nothing binding between you. But, if you say, 'Yes, I will take your information on then Square,' then, remember that what you hear is your Brother Master Mason's secret, and must not be passed on to another Brother Master Mason by you, even under a similar bond of secrecy.

If, however, the information you have received Masonically, or on the Square, refers to such matters as murder, treason, or such like acts against the laws of God and man, you are exempt from the binding of your secrecy and it is left to your own discretion as to what you may make of the information.

The seventh clause needs no explanation. We hand it on to you as it is given to us, but I would strongly impress upon you that for the violation of this clause the punishment is total expulsion for the Order of Freemasonry.

You have promised to observe this Obligation by bearing in mind the ancient penalty, and binding yourself under the real penalty of being deservedly branded as a wretch, base, faithless and unfit for the society of men of honour, should you ever violate this solemn obligation of a Master Mason.

You no doubt will have noticed many points in the conferring of this degree which are different from your previous degrees, but there is one outstanding difference in this degree to which I especially call attention; that is, in your former degrees you were assisted to rise from the altar on being given the Secret Word and Grip, but on this occasion you were assisted to rise on being given the Pass Word and Grip. Now, that is not an error on our part, there is a reason for it, and the reason will be explained in what is known as the Legend of the Degree, wherein you will learn how, by the untimely death of a certain man, the means of communicating the Secret Word was at an end and eventually the Word itself became lost. You will learn how a new Word was substituted, and the method of communicating the information. I shall now recite to you the Legend of the Degree.

Note:—Prior to admitting the Candidate into the Lodge room, the 'Cloth' should be placed in position on the floor. The Master and Wardens come forward, armed with the heavy implements referred to in the Legend. The Junior Warden stands on the Candidate's right, the Senior Warden on the Candidate's left, and the Worshipful Master stands in front of the Candidate.

The Candidate, supported by the Wardens, is placed in the peculiar position and remains so until that point in the Legend when he assumes another position.

THE LEGEND OF THE DEGREE

COND.—We read in the Volume of the Sacred Law that on a certain day, David King of Israel, sitting in his palace and mediating on matters concerning his people. brought to mind the fact that which he, the King, dwelt in a beautiful house of Cedar wood, yet the Ark of the Covenant and the Shekinah which represented the presence of JEHOVAH had for its habitation the tabernacle, a tent-like and moveable structure. The King considered that this was not right or seemly and determined that he would build a magnificent Temple as a proper dwelling place for the Ark, and where the Glory of the LORD might abide forever.

Accordingly, he made out plans for the intended building and gave instructions for the gathering of large quantities of gold, silver, precious stones and the like.

But the word of the Lord was conveyed to him by the prophet Nathan saying that he, the King. would not be permitted to undertake this work as he had been engaged in warfare and so his hands were stained with blood, but that his son, Solomon, would be entrusted with the work when he should be ascend the throne of Israel. King David bowed to the will of the Almighty and in due time was gathered to his forefathers.

In the fourth year of the reign of King Solomon, the land of Israel had peace, having for some time being subdued the warlike nations round its borders, and King Solomon was not forgetful of the wish of his father, nor the promise of the Almighty, and set about preparing for the building of the Great Temple.

Now the Israelites were an agricultural and pastoral people, and had little skill in the art of building, and Solomon knowing this was aware that it would be necessary to look for assistance outside his dominion. He remembered that a neighboring monarch. King Hiram of Tyre, had been very friendly towards his father David, whom he had assisted in building his own palace, and as at that time the Phoenicians were renowned for their skill in architecture and building King Solomon determined to approach King Hiram of Tyre. and asked for his assistance on this occasion.

When King Hiram received the messengers from King Solomon, and heard the request, he gladly promised to do all that was asked of him because of the love that he had for King David.

He therefore commanded his servants to go up to the forests of Lebanon, and there cut down cedar trees, which were conveyed in floats or rafts to the seaport town of Joppa, which port was most convenient Jerusalem. King Hiram also sent his skilled Craftsmen to cut and carve the timber, and also to prepare the stone for the intended building and to instruct the men of Israel in that art. In return for this great kindness, King Solomon gave to King Hiram gifts of corn, oil, and wine.

The number of workers engaged in the preparation for the building was 153,300 and King Solomon considered it would be advisable to have one man who should act as Chief Architect or Overseer, to direct the Workers and to see that the work was being carried out according to the design and plan. He again sent to King Hiram for advice and help, and King Hiram sent him a man who proved in every way fit and capable for the position.

This man was also called Hiram, a skilled and cunning craftsman. He was known as the 'widow's son.' His father had been a Tyrian and his mother an Israelite of the tribe of Naphtali.

This Hiram was greatly respected by King Hiram of Tyre and was given the title of ABIF, one of great reverence meaning, 'my father.'

The workers were divided into three classes or grades: First, those who did the rough work of hewing the timber and stone; second, those who being more skilled brought the material to the required size and shape; and, thirdly, the Master Craftsmen or Overseers who finally passed the material for its appointed place in the building.

All the work was prepared so that the timber and stone should take its place without the sound of axe or hammer, or the use of any iron tool.

In reciting this Legend, we give our modern terms to these three grades, and so refer to them as Entered Apprentices, Fellowcrafts, and Master Masons.

Over this vast army of workers King Solomon, King Hiram, and Hiram Abif constituted themselves as what we would call Grand Masters, and acted as a court of appeal in all matters of differences and difficulties arising among the workers. To mark their authority they each wore a golden Square on their breast.

The wages paid to the workers were as follows:—to the first grade, or Entered Apprentices in kind, such as corn, oil, etc.; to the second or Fellowcrafts, partly in kind and money; and to the third or Master Masons, entirely in money, so it will be readily understood that it was the natural ambition of those of the first and second grades to qualify as quickly as possible for that of the higher grade of Master Mason, and so receive the higher remuneration.

To each grade of workers was given a secret word, and on applying to the paymasters for payment, the workers gave the secret word of his particular grade or degree, and was paid accordingly.

So highly did King Solomon, King Hiram and Hiram Abif regard the grade of Master Mason that they made a solemn agreement between themselves to the effect that only in their presence could the secret word of the Master Mason be communicated to a craftsman when being advanced to that degree.

The building was drawing near its completion and fifteen craftsmen of the Fellowcraft class were fearful that the temple would be finished before they advanced to the Master Mason degree, and thus lose payment in wages. They therefore formed a conspiracy amongst themselves with the object of finding the secret word of a Master Mason and three of them, so very desperate and determined, stated that they were prepared to commit murder if by so doing it should help them to gain their desire. The remaining twelve were not prepared to go to such an extreme measure, and withdrew from the conspiracy.

At High Noon it was customary for the workers to rest from their labours for the mid-day meal, and Hiram Abif spent this hour of quiet and rest within the partially completed building for meditation.

The three conspirators were aware of the practice, and knowing that the Grand Master was thus cut off and isolated from the general body of workers, they considered he was the very person whom they should approach, and at all costs obtain from him the information they so earnestly desired. Arming themselves with heavy implements, one with the 24-inch Gauge, one with the Square, and the third with the Maul, they waited outside the gates of the courtyard of the Temple, one at the South gate, one at the West gate, and the third at the East gate.

When Hiram Abif sought to leave the precincts of the Temple by the South gate he was confronted by the first conspirator who demanded from him the secret word of a Master Mason. The Grand Master reasoned with him saying that no so had he received the word and therefore could not communicate it but urged the Craftsman to work on diligently and with patience, and no doubt in due time he would receive his reward. Annoyed at not receiving the information, the conspirator struck the Grand Master a blow across the throat with the 24-inch Gauge. Alarmed by this sudden attack, the Grand Master at once closed the gate and proceeded to seek an exit by the Western gate, but here he was met by the second conspirator who likewise demanded the secret word of a Master Mason. With him Hiram Abif remonstrated and urged him not to seek the information by such rash or unlawful means. Enraged by this refusal the conspirator struck a blow on the left breast with the Square. Hastily closing the Western gate the Grand Master made his way to the Eastern gate as the final means of escape, and on crossing the courtyard he became faint with the double attack (*here explain the first by-Sign, or that of Anguish*). Having arrived at the Eastern gate he was met by the third conspirator who roughly demanded from him the secret word of a Master Mason. The Grand Master, still unshaken in his purpose firmly refused to give the information, saying, 'Not so have I received it and I would rather die than give it unlawfully.' On receiving this answer to his request, the conspirator raised the heavy Maul and struck the Grand Master a violent blow on the forehead and said, 'Then die!' (*The symbolic meaning of the Candidate's position is now explained.*)

Finding that the Grand Master was slain, the conspirators removed the body and gave it a rough and rude burial. They then fled from Jerusalem.

Owing to the absence of Hiram Abif, confusion arose amongst the Craftsmen, as no instructions were forthcoming, and fearing that the Grand Master had met his death at the hands of the three conspirators, the other twelve who had withdrawn from the original agreement went to King Solomon and told him what they suspected.

King Solomon immediately ordered that parties should be sent out to see if any trace or tidings could be obtained as to what had befallen the Grand Master, and also to seek for the Murderers, and if these men were found they should be brought before him. Three search parties set out. One party going Southward returned after a few days without any tidings. A second search part going Westward eventually reached the sea coast at Joppa, and there they gave up hope of any further search fearing that the assassins had probably left the country by ship. While considering what to do, they heard to their amazement, the sound of voices coming as if out of the ground, and on investigating closely they discovered that the sounds came from one of the caves on the foreshore. Listening intently they heard a voice exclaim, 'Woe is me! Would that my throat had been cut across, the tongue torn out at the root and buried in the rough sands of the sea, a Cable Tow's length from the shore, where the tide ebbs and flows twice daily, ere I had conspired against our good and great Grand Master.'

A second voice exclaimed, 'Woe, woe is me! Would that my left breast had been torn open, my heart plucked from thence, and thrown as a prey to the birds of the air, ere I had conspired against our good and great Grand Master.'

And again a third voice was heard saying, 'Woe, woe, woe! A triple woe is mine! Would that my body had been sawn in twain, my bowels taken therefrom, and with my body burned to ashes and the ashes scattered to the four winds of heaven, so that no trace of such a vile wretch might be found, for it was my right hand that struck the blow that killed our good and great Grand Master.'

On hearing these confession the search party rushed into the cave where they found the assassins, whom they quickly overpowered, bound them, and brought them before King Solomon, who ordered that the penalties severally invoked should be meted out to the murderers.

The third search party, after a fruitless search, at length returned to Jerusalem. They rested a while considering what report they should make to King Solomon. Having come to an agreement, and preparing to go to the King, one of the party, in assisting himself to arise, caught hold of a shrub nearby, which, to his amazement, came away loosely from the earth. Calling the attention of his Brethren to this unusual occurrence, they examined the ground closely and concluded it was probably the hastily made grave of some unclean person or animal. To mark the spot they placed over it a sprig of Acacia, which would also serve as a warning to passers by, and thus prevent defilement to the Priest and Levite, according to the law of Moses.

Fearing the worst, they went to King Solomon and reported what they had discovered. On hearing the news, the King ordered them to return to the supposed grave, examine its contents, and if by any chance it should contain the body of the missing Grand Master, they should raise the body and bring it to a place for more decent and fitting interment. The King also instructed them to take particular notice of any unusual actions, Words or Signs, which might be made by those watching the opening of the grave, as by the untimely death of Hiram Abif the means of communicating the secrets of a Master Mason were now at an end, and thus new Words, Signs, and the manner of communicating the same would have to be substituted.

The search party returned to the supposed grave and at once proceeded to investigate its contents.

On removing some of the clay the head of a corpse was disclosed showing a deep wound in the forehead. On seeing this the bystanders all touched their foreheads, *etc. (Sign of Sympathy explained. This is the second by-Sign in Freemasonry.)*

Removing more of the clay, a stench arose owing to decomposition of the body, which caused those assembled to turn aside thus: (*Sign of Horror explained. This is the third by-Sign in Freemasonry.*)

On removing all the covering the searchers discovered the Golden Square on the breast of the corpse, which left no doubt in their minds as to the identity of the body, and on seeing this some of the party exclaimed, 'Alas, the Builder!' and throwing up their hands, *etc.* (*Grand Hailing Sign and words given*).

To raise the body one of the Craftsmen stepped into the grave, and attempted to raise it by giving the Entered Apprentice Grip, but owing to decomposition the flesh came away, and the hand dropped to the side. (*This is known as the 'first slip' in Freemasonry.*)

A second Craftsman entered and endeavored to raise it by means of the Grip of a Fellowcraft, but against the flesh came away, letting the hand fall to the side. (*This is known as the 'second slip' in Freemasonry.*)

Finally, an experienced Craftsman entered the grave and, taking the hand of the corpse with the grip known as the —— raised the body from the dead level to the living upright, as I now raise you; and I raise you on the Five Points of Fellowship.

The Candidate is now raised on the Five Points of Fellowship. In this position the secret Substituted Word is given. The Conductor then explains the Five Points of Fellowship, the by-Signs and the Grand Hailing Sign; after which, he proceeds:—

COND.—If undergoing an examination proving yourself a Master Mason you may be asked the following questions: 'Wherefrom, whereto, whereon and whereunder were you raised?'

You will answer: 'From the dead level to the living upright, on the Five Points of Fellowship, under the Warrant of the Lodge.'

You are now a Master Mason, and therefore entitled to enjoy all the rights and privileges according to that rank in Freemasonry. You may now take part in all matters concerning the Lodge, and speak your opinion on all points which may be under discussion for the welfare of the lodge in particular and Freemasonry in general.

You have the right to propose Candidates for membership; but with regard to the proposal of Candidates, we ask you to use discretion, and never insist on the proposal of any Candidate who may not prove acceptable to your Brethren, thus preserving the Peace, Love and Harmony of the Lodge.

You have the right of visiting any regular Masonic Lodge under any Constitution of Freemasonry in friendly communication with the Grand Lodge of Ireland—subject, of course, to being able to prove yourself a Master Mason to the satisfaction of the Brethren of the Lodge whom you intend to visit, and the permission of the Worshipful Master of the particular Lodge to admit you to the meeting.

You are permitted to attend meetings of the Grand Lodge of Ireland, all provincial Grand Lodge meetings, and the Grand lodge of Instruction.

You will receive, in due course, a certificate from the Grand Lodge of Ireland declaring you to be a Master Mason, which you will sign in the presence of your Brethren in Open Lodge. This certificate will prove helpful to you when you are a visitor at a Lodge where you are not known, or cannot be vouched, as before you could be admitted you would have to undergo an examination in the presence of at least three Brethren of the Lodge proving yourself a Master Mason and, on signing your name in the visitors' book your signature in that book would be compared with your signature on the certificate.

In the Irish Constitution the procedure of entry into a Lodge meeting after the meeting has been opened, and you are vouched or made known to the Tyler, is as follows:—

The Tyler gives the knocks on the door according to whatever degree the Lodge may be working on at the moment. When it is convenient to open the door, the knocks will be repeated by the Inner Guard from within. The door is then opened, and you are announced by the Tyler. The door is closed, and the Inner Guard makes due announcement to the

Worshipful Master. If your admission is acceptable, the door will be opened and you will be invited to enter.

On your entry you will give the Inner Guard the Entrance Phrase or Pass Word according to the degree on which the Lodge is at labour, then advance to the centre of the room in front of the altar facing the Worshipful Master and stand to order on the degree on which the Lodge is working.

In some Lodges under the Irish Constitution it is customary for the Worshipful Master to challenge the visitor, and he may say, 'Whence come you, Brother?' You will reply, 'From the West, Worshipful Master.' The Worshipful Master may then ask, ' What tidings do you bring?' Your answer will be, 'Peace, Love and harmony to all good and true Masons, but especially to the Worshipful Master, Wardens and Brethren of this Lodge.' The Worshipful Master would then ask you to be seated when you would complete the Salute and take a seat in the body of the Lodge.

In the event of not being so challenged, you would salute the Worshipful Master and be seated. This challenging is not usual in our Sister Constitutions.

At the close of a Lodge meeting there is an opportunity given to convey fraternal greetings when the Worshipful Master asks, 'Has any visiting Brother anything to say for the good of Freemasonry in general or this Lodge in particular?' You would rise, salute and say, 'Fraternal greetings from Lodge — —', giving the number of your own Lodge, and if you should be a visitor at any of the Lodges under the jurisdiction of any other Constitution, you would add the words 'Irish Constitution.'

I will now explain the position of the Three Great Lights which are changed according to the degree on which the Lodge is at labour.

On the degree of Entered Apprentice you will notice the Square and Compasses are in this position: (*explained by Conductor: both points of Compasses under the Square*). symbolising the hidden points of our secrets.

On the degree of Fellowcraft the position is thus (*explained by Conductor: one point of Compasses over one arm of the Square*), illustrating the 'Beginning of Knowledge'; and on this degree of Master Mason, with the Compasses over the Square, signifies that you have received all the secrets of Craft Masonry.

WORKING TOOLS

The Working Tools applied to this degree are the Pencil, the Skirret, and the Compasses.

The Pencil is used by the Operative Master Mason in drawing or tracing designs for intended buildings, recording work done, and giving an account of the behaviour of Operatives under his charge. Thus, the Pencil symbolically reminds the Speculative Mason that his words and actions are recorded by the Almighty Architect to whom, at some time, he must give an account of his action and conduct through his mortal life.

The Skirret is an implement which acts on a centre pin, from which a line is unwound. The line is chalked, and struck on the ground to mark out the plan for an intended building. So the Skirret reminds us of the straight and undeviating line of conduct marked out for us in the Volume of the Sacred Law.

The Compasses is an implement consisting of two moveable legs hinged together at one end, used for describing circles, and by the Architect for measuring figures in preparing his plans, and enables him to give his designs the just proportions which will insure Beauty as well as Stability in his work. So in Speculative Masonry, this implement is symbolic of Virtue, that true standard of rectitude which alone can bestow happiness here and felicity hereafter.

The Candidate is now brought before the Worshipful Master and invested with the appropriate Apron. He is then placed in the Northeast corner of the Lodge Room while the Charge is read to him.

CHARGE TO THE MASTER MASON

Brother, your zeal for the principles of Freemasonry, your progress in their practical application, and your obedience to our general regulations, have pointed you out as a fit object of esteem and advancement.

In the character of a Master Mason you are henceforth authorised to warn the younger Brethren against conduct tending to any breach of fidelity, and to bring all irregular work into conformity with the general plan of Freemasonry. You are to inculcate universal benevolence and, by the propriety of your own behaviour, to afford the best example for the conduct of others. The Ancient Landmarks of the Craft are to be your constant care, and you are to preserve them sacred and inviolate and never to sanction any infringement of our customs or a deviation from established usages.

Duty, honour and gratitude now bind you to your trust; let no motive, therefore, ever make you swerve from your voluntary Obligations. Imitate, rather, the example of that true and trusty Craftsman whom you have once represented. Endeavor, in a word, to convince the world that merit alone has been your title to our confidence, and that on you our privileges have been deservedly bestowed.

The Candidate is now seated in the Northeast corner and saluted.

CALLING DOWN FROM AN
M.M. TO F.C.

WM—Brother Secretary, have you any further business for transaction on this degree?

SECY—Worshipful Master, there is no further business for consideration.

WM— ●| Rise, Brethren, and assist me to call down the Lodge.

WM— ●| — ●| ●|

SW— ●| — ●| ●|

JW— ●| — ●| ●|

WM—Brother Junior Warden, what is the first care of a Master in calling down the Lodge?

WM—See that duty performed.

JW—Brother Inner Guard, see that the Lodge is tyled.

IG— ●| — ●| ●|

TYLER— ●| — ●| ●|

IG—*Opens the door.*

TYLER—Brother Inner Guard, the Lodge is tyled.

IG—(*Closes the door*) Brother Junior Warden, the Lodge is tyled.

JW—Worshipful Master, the Lodge is tyled.

WM—Let the Wardens declare to the Brethren that it is my will and pleasure that the Lodge do now resume Labour.

SW—Brethren, it is the will and pleasure of the Worshipful Master that the Lodge do now resume Labour.

JW—Brethren, it is the will and pleasure of the Worshipful Master that the Lodge do now resume Labour.

WM—Accordingly, Brethren, in the Name of the Most High God, The Great God of the Universe, I declare the Lodge to be now at Labour on the Second or Fellowcraft Degree of Freemasonry, for the transaction of all such business as may be regularly brought before it; your Pass Word being '—' and this — (*making the sign*) your True Guard and Sign.

WM— ●| — ●| ●|

SW— ●| — ●| ●|

71

SW—⊸⊨ – ⊸⊨ ⊸⊨
JW—⊸⊨ – ⊸⊨ ⊸⊨
IG—⊸⊨ – ⊸⊨ ⊸⊨
TYLER—⊸⊨ – ⊸⊨ ⊸⊨
BRN—*Salute and sit down.*

While the Wardens are declaring 'the will and pleasure of the Worshipful Master,' the Director of Ceremonies ALONE goes before the Altar, and when the Worshipful Master declares 'the Lodge to be now at Labour' on the Fellowcraft Degree, the Director of Ceremonies will arrange the Three Great Lights accordingly.

CPSIA information can be obtained
at www.ICGtesting.com
Printed in the USA
BVHW090739090921
616333BV00009B/850

9 781162 568454